CODEX:
EYE OF TERROR

Written by
Andy Chambers, Pete Haines, Andy Hoare, Phil Kelly & Graham McNeill.

Cover Art
Karl Kopinski

Graphics
Nuala Kennedy, Stefan Kopinski & Neil Hodgson.

Production
Mark Owen & Nathan Winter.

Internal Art
Alex Boyd, David Gallagher,
Paul Jeacock, Karl Kopinski,
Paul Dainton & John Wigley.

Miniatures Designers
Tim Adcock, Mark Bedford,
Jes Goodwin, Brian Nelson,
Alan Perry & Michael Perry.

Miniatures Painters
Kev Asprey, Neil Green, Tammy Haye,
Darren Latham, Kirsten Mickelburgh,
Seb Perbet & Keith Robertson.

The Imperium faces its greatest challenge in ten millennia. The Arch Heretic, Abaddon the Despoiler, has forged a fearsome alliance of Chaos Space Marine legions, deviants, traitors, foul mutants and daemons to hurl against the Imperium. The fate of Humanity rests on the desperate battles being fought around the Eye of Terror and the garrison world of Cadia, home of the famed Cadian regiments of the Imperial Guard. The Emperor's loyal servants have resisted Abaddon's Black Crusades in the past, but always at a terrible cost. Can they prevent this Thirteenth Crusade, the greatest so far, from breaching the Cadian Gate to assail the very heart of the Imperium – ancient Terra?

Codex: Eye of Terror breaks down as follows:

A Sector of Unending War. The history of the Cadian Sector and the Eye of Terror, Abaddon's previous crusades, the Gothic War and the individuals who have made this one of the most fought-over sectors in the Imperium. In addition,

you'll find details of the many and varied forces currently fighting around the Eye of Terror and read of the terrible events that have led to the horror of Abaddon's Thirteenth Black Crusade.

The Colours of War. These colour pages show many painted examples of the superb miniatures that can be used to fight battles in the Eye of Terror campaign. You'll also find ideas for converting your own models as well as photos showing examples of the different kinds of battlefields being fought over by the various forces.

Army List Variants. The four army list variants included in this book allow you to collect and game with some of the different forces fighting in and around the Eye of Terror. Based upon existing codexes, these lists allow you to field the disciplined forces of the Cadian regiments, a Strike Force from the Ulthwé Craftworld, the shambling hordes of the Lost and the Damned or howling packs of the Space Wolves 13th Company.

CONTENTS

PRODUCED BY GAMES WORKSHOP

British Cataloguing-in-Publication Data. A catalogue record for this book is available from the British Library.

PRODUCT CODE: 60 03 01 99 007   Games Workshop World Wide Web site: http://www.games-workshop.com   ISBN: 1-84154-398-5

"Since the time of The Fall,
our race has been haunted by what we,
in our reckless pursuit of hedonistic indulgence,
gave birth to. Though our dreams once overturned
worlds and quenched suns, we are now but fitful
shadows clinging to the edge of existence. All the stars in
the sky cannot blot out the hateful glare of the Red Moon's
Eye. The birthing place of The Great Enemy pulses with all the
malice of a daemon that is dreaming, casting its shadow over
all we have ever done and all we ever shall. Every twisted strand
of Fate and casting of the Runes leads me to this time, to this
place, and it is clear that the final battle awaits me at the ancient
Crone Worlds. A conflict the likes of which has not been seen
since the Mon-Keigh warred amongst themselves, and their corpse
of a seer fell to his traitorous son, is coming and all my steps lead
towards it, no matter that I walk other paths. I see the stars
stained red with the blood of the Mon-Keigh and, though their
wars do not concern me and I would gladly let them destroy one
another, I know that to avoid this fight is to condemn my race
to inevitable doom. And though all I see is darkness, I know
that I will not flinch from my destiny."

Eldrad Ulthran –
Farseer of Ulthwé Craftworld

HISTORY OF THE CADIAN GATE

Gateway to the Eye of Terror

To fully understand the Cadian people and their way of life, it is necessary to go back ten thousand years to a time lost in legend, a time of war and blood known as the Horus Heresy. The Emperor and his progeny, the Primarchs, stood shoulder to shoulder and carved a realm amongst the stars in a time of heroes. Each Primarch led a Legion of the Emperor's finest soldiers, genetically enhanced warriors known as the Space Marines, and fought battles beyond number to liberate human space from the clutches of aliens, Chaos and all manner of terrible foes. Each of the Primarchs was a superhuman figure, gods amongst men, but like men they could also be prey to jealousy, bitterness and vanity. Such was the fate of Warmaster Horus, the Emperor's most favoured son and Primarch of the Luna Wolves.

Chaos had corrupted Horus, so subtly and gradually that he had not recognised his descent into evil until it had already consumed him. Such was Horus's skill in manipulating others to do his bidding, that he corrupted fully half of the Legions to his cause and led them in rebellion against the Emperor. As hostilities erupted, it became clear that the rot had spread much further than anyone could have believed possible, as regiment after regiment of the Imperial Guard declared for Horus. The Collegias of the Adeptus Mechanicus split apart in rebellion and entire Titan Legions unfurled banners with the blasphemous runes of the Chaos gods upon them. Horus attacked without mercy, driving the forces of his once-brother Space Marines before him. Before long, Horus's advance had breached the heart of the Emperor's realm; his warships had defeated Battlefleet Solar and smashed the lunar defences, leaving Terra virtually unprotected.

The hordes of Chaos landed on the holy soil of Terra, traitor Space Marines, shambling mutants and cultists beyond number. The battle raged for many weeks, with the death toll spiralling into the millions. Everywhere, the forces of the Emperor were pushed back, choking the halls of the Imperial Palace with dead as they fought for every yard of ground. Eventually, the traitors breached the final walls of the palace and the end looked certain. Horus was a master strategist, but it was at this point that he made a fatal error. Knowing that Imperial reinforcements in the shape of the Dark Angels and Space Wolves were nearing, he knew he had to end the siege of the Emperor's Palace soon. Horus moved his battle barge into low orbit and ordered its shields lowered. Whether this was a reckless gamble or the last of Horus's humanity surfacing will never be known, but, faced with such an opportunity, the Emperor could not afford to miss this chance to take the fight to Horus.

The Emperor and two of his most devoted Primarchs, Sanguinius of the Blood Angels and Rogal Dorn of the Imperial Fists, teleported onto Horus's flagship with their most trusted warriors. They found a craft warped by the powers of Chaos, barely recognisable as having been forged by human hands. Diabolical sorceries scattered the Emperor's force throughout the ship and when the Emperor finally came face to face with Horus, he found the Warmaster standing above the broken body of Sanguinius. The Emperor fought Horus in every way imaginable – physically, spiritually and psychically – with the war-torn planet below as the prize for the victor. The battle was long, but eventually, the Emperor was able to defeat Horus, though it was at the cost of much of his humanity. At the battle's conclusion, the Emperor's body was little more than a broken shell. Rogal Dorn found the Emperor's shattered body and returned him to Earth, whereupon he ascended to the Golden Throne that sustains his life force to this very day.

The defeated Traitor forces collapsed with the death of Horus and fled in disarray from the gates of Terra that had proved to be just beyond their grasp. Some loyalist forces rallied and gave chase, but most remained on Terra to consolidate their great victory. Many rebels were put to the sword, but the majority of the Traitor Legions escaped to the realm of space known as the Eye of Terror, that region of space where reality and insanity collide and the raw energy of the Warp pours into realspace in a swirling maelstrom. Here, the gods of Chaos rule over uncounted planets, all warped to their own evil aspects, and this is where the Traitor Legions found refuge from their pursuers, isolated from the galaxy by powerful Warp storms.

Each world within the Eye of Terror is a daemon world, warped and twisted by the whims of the gods of Chaos and the powerful daemon princes who rule them. The Traitor Legions regrouped and nurtured their hatred, planning for the day when they would wreak a terrible vengeance on those who had defied them. Within the Eye, time flows differently. Those same traitors who fought on Terra still fight in the service of their monstrous gods. They fight against each other to prove their supremacy, and against the forces of the Imperium when the Warp storms calm long enough to allow them to rampage into Imperial space. The sectors surrounding the Eye of Terror are heavily militarised to resist these invasions when they come, and none more so than Cadia, the fortress world that stands at the mouth of the one stable route leading from the Eye of Terror, the Cadian Gate.

Fortress Cadia

Cadia stands upon the one reliable route to and from the Eye of Terror and, as such, is one of the most strategically vital worlds in the Imperium. There are other routes from the Eye, but none are as stable as the Cadian Gate, and no force of any size can venture forth from the Eye without first passing through it. The exact reasons for this calm area of space is uncertain, though many believe it is due to the presence of the famous Cadian Pylons. These mysterious black monoliths dot the landscape of Cadia, and their origins have remained unexplained since Cadia was first settled by humans.

Cadia itself is a bleak, merciless and wind-blown planet, where only the strongest survive to adulthood and discipline is learned at the earliest age. Cold winds howl across wide, sundered plains where armies train with live ammunition and every day not spent training is a day wasted. Every city, or Kasr, is a fortress, with the streets and buildings fashioned with great cunning by the finest military architects. Every Cadian is taught the skills of the warrior as soon as they can walk and they are much sought after by commanders throughout the galaxy. Such a planet breeds hardy and determined warriors and the Cadian regiments have a well-deserved reputation for both honour and fighting spirit. From the earliest age, Cadians are taught to field strip a weapon with their eyes shut and tactical doctrine is taught before reading and writing. One soldier in every ten is recruited into the Interior Guard, regardless of ability or achievements, and as a result some of the most able soldiers spend their entire military service on Cadia and the soldiers of the Cadian Planetary Defence Force are amongst the most effective and skilled fighting men in the Imperium.

The pylon had been looming in our windscreen for a while now, and Fischig swept us around it, almost kissing the black stone. The moaning song of the wind as it laced through the geometries of the pylon was now so loud I could hear it over the racing turbines of the speeder.

The pylon was vast: half a kilometre high and a quarter square. The upper facing of the smooth black stone was machined with delicate craft to form holes and other round-edged orifices no bigger than a man's head. It was through these slim, two hundred and fifty metre tubes that the wind moaned and howled.

And the tubes weren't straight. They wove through the pylon like worm tunnels. Tech-magi had tried running tiny servitor probes through them to map their loops, but generally the probes didn't come back.

As we banked up higher for another pass, I could see the distant shape of the neighbouring pylon, across the moors, sixty kilometres away. Five thousand, eight hundred and ten known pylons dot the surface of Cadia, not counting the two thousand others that remain as partial ruins or buried relics.

No two are identical in design. Each one rises to a precise half kilometre height and is sunk a quarter kilometre into the ground. They predate mankind's arrival in this system, and their manner of manufacture is unknown. They are totally inert, by any auspex measure known to our race, but many believe their presence explains the quieting of the violent warp torrents that makes the Cadian Gate the single, calm, navigable route to the Ocularis Terribus.

Excerpted from the novel *Malleus* by Dan Abnett.
Used courtesy of the Black Library.

The training I undertook upon my assignment to the 122nd Cadian Regiment was different from the normal activities involved in most regimental training I had thus far undergone in my career with the Imperial Commissariat. My initial surprise was the youth of my companions in the basic training program, all of whom were much, much younger than myself, the oldest being perhaps fourteen. I had heard that the Cadians began their training young, but frankly, this astonished me, though not as much as the level of competence displayed by such youngsters. At first I was indignant at being forced to train with children, but I was soon to be disabused of this notion after witnessing their fitness and skill at arms.

There were many specialised skills I needed to learn very quickly in order to operate with the Cadians, and the emphasis was very definitely on improving my stamina and overall strength. For too long I had ridden in the cupola of a Chimera and the first days of training were harder than any battle I have fought in. But I was determined to uphold the honour of my position and refused to fail. In short, after three months I could run, jump and fight for prodigious distances carrying a significant weight. Such activities required special determination and failure is not an option for troopers in the Cadian Regiments. As a newly assigned Commissar, I had to perform doubly well to earn the respect of the soldiers.

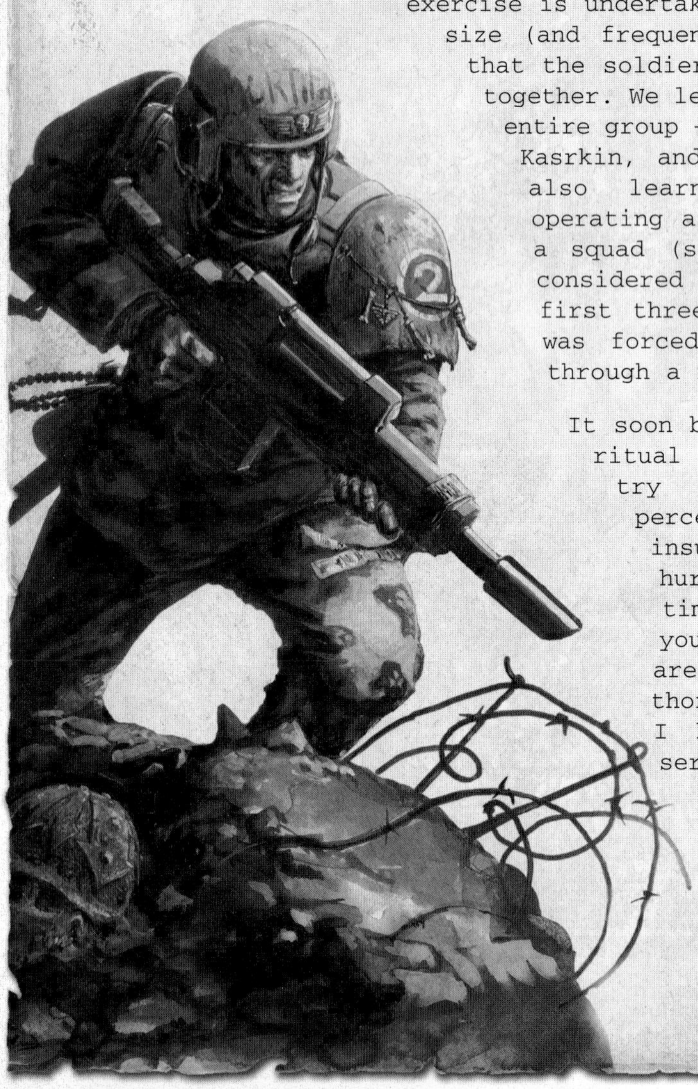

One of the biggest factors in the Cadian training program is learning to function as a team. Every challenge and exercise is undertaken in groups of at least squad size (and frequently larger) and it is crucial that the soldiers learn to operate effectively together. We learned how to move at pace as an entire group – known as speed marching in the Kasrkin, and something of an art form. We also learned the difference between operating as an individual and as part of a squad (something I had not previously considered valuable). Many times during my first three months I almost faltered and was forced to rely on my squad to get through a number of challenges.

It soon became clear to me that it is a ritual amongst the Cadian troopers to try and outperform anyone they perceive as an outsider, and this insular nature was one of the many hurdles I had to overcome in my time with the 122nd. But say what you will about the Cadians, they are amongst the strongest and most thoroughly disciplined formations I have ever had the honour of serving with.

Excerpted from the memoirs of
Commissar Kotarian Verhek,
assigned to the
122nd Cadian Regiment 963.M41

Like many sector-wide conflicts, the Gothic war began slowly, with sporadic, and seemingly insignificant, raids against smaller outposts (qv. The Arx Raid). Vessels stricken with disease were discovered adrift in the Athena Sector, along with sightings of the Chaos vessel *Plagueclaw*, and Astropaths began reporting unsettling disturbances in the Warp. Panic and anarchy became widespread as fanatical sects arose, believing that the Emperor, bless his holy name, was displeased with them. Hysteria spread throughout the sector and on many worlds order broke down completely. The Imperial Navy lost several ships to 'accidents' in space dock that were subsequently blamed on poor maintenance and faulty ammunition – a rather too convenient explanation for my tastes. Three years after the first raid at Arx, the forces of the Despoiler struck.

Abaddon's fleets struck at a dozen Imperial bases and sent the warships of Battlefleet Gothic reeling. Chaos ships attacked all across the Gothic Sector and the first inkling of Abaddon's true intentions was to come to light in the Rebo system, where one of the mysterious Blackstone Fortresses orbited the fifth planet. These massive edifices of unknown origin had been refitted to serve as bases for the ships of Battlefleet Gothic. For the first time in history, one of these fell to Abaddon's forces, and he was soon to make horrifying use of the captured base.

Abaddon's fleet had a devastating weapon, never before seen, named the *Planet Killer*. Its name was not simply born from the arrogance of its builders, but horrifyingly well deserved, as Abaddon demonstrated at the Cardinal world of Savaven. The account of the destruction of Savaven from Jeremiah Soldagen, Savaven's orbital defence commander, still has the power to chill the soul. His description of continents splitting apart, burning skies and the planet breaking into pieces makes solemn reading indeed. Fourteen million people died within an hour and the crippling effects of this on Imperial morale should not be underestimated; many worlds were hurriedly – though unfortunately not entirely – evacuated before the *Planet Killer* arrived.

Another Blackstone fell at Brinaga. At Fularis II, Abaddon was to terrifyingly demonstrate the true power of these ancient constructs.

Exact information regarding the incident is sketchy, but evidence points to a massive energy beam being unleashed from the Blackstone Fortress that scoured Fularis II bare, stripping its atmosphere and transforming its surface into a barren, rocky plain.

Imperial forces were continually engaged throughout the sector, from the Hammerhead Deeps to the Cyclops Cluster, desperate to halt the might of the Chaos fleet. At the outset of 151.M41, Lord Admiral Ravensburg took the fight to the enemy, resulting in the clash at Gethsemane where he was able to utterly destroy a Chaos fleet of considerable size. Eldar vessels also fought in this battle, though many historians believe their role to have been minimal, whereas my researches – particularly into the actions of Captain Leoten Semper and his ship, the *Lord Solar Macharius* – point to a considerable Eldar involvement in the latter stages of the war (qv. Warp Gates).

News of this great victory invigorated the Imperial Navy and, as the Warp storms that had isolated the Gothic Sector for so long began to abate, vessels from neighbouring sectors were finally able to reinforce the Lord Admiral's bloodied fleet. Abaddon brought the full power of the Blackstones to bear on the star of Tarantis, the mustering point for ships entering the Gothic Sector, in an attempt to stem Ravensburg's reinforcements. Combining their power, the Blackstones caused the Tarantis star to explode, killing everything still within the system.

The final battle of the war was to be fought at Shindelgeist, where Blackstone V floated in the depths of space. A trap was sprung by the Lord Admiral and the Eldar, who defeated Abaddon's greatest fleet in a truly magnificent three-day battle. In an act of spite, Abaddon sought to destroy the star there also, and had it not been for the sacrifice of Captain Abridal on the *Flame of Purity*, the victory would have been a hollow one. Abaddon had been defeated, though he escaped with two of his captured Blackstones, though various sources claim that they must have been destroyed. Unfortunately, this appears to be merely wishful thinking; while the ultimate fate of these immeasurably powerful artefacts is as yet unknown, I fear the Imperium will eventually rue their loss.

The Imperial Fleet of Lord Admiral Ravensburg defeats Abaddon's forces at Shindelgeist

CREEPING DEATH

As the end of the forty-first millennium drew closer, the first signs that Abaddon's long-feared attack was imminent came in the form of numerous sightings of drifting vessels emerging from the Warp in the surrounding sectors. All were converging on the core systems of each sub sector and, while this number of space hulks was rare, it was not unheard of. System defence ships scrambled to intercept them and prevent them from reaching their systems' inhabited worlds. The vessels of the Adeptus Astartes boarded those they could, but their numbers were limited. The Space Marines found them to be twisted and disease-ridden nightmares, encrusted with all manner of necrotic matter and toxic filth. Subsequently, every such vessel encountered was destroyed with torpedoes and bombardment cannons, but for some it was already too late.

With a synchronicity that could not have been coincidence, outbreaks of virulent sickness erupted among Imperial Navy crews within a day of a reported sighting of the dreaded Chaos vessel *Plagueclaw* in the outer reaches of the Urthwart system by Captain Roark of the Dauntless class cruiser *Duke Lurstophan*. As the sickness spread throughout the region's naval forces, and the number of ships fit for duty fell exponentially, even more hulks dropped from the Warp, converging on vital strategic worlds. Ships from neighbouring sub sectors rushed to destroy the hulks and a small, ad hoc fleet was assembled at Belis Corona under the command of Admiral Quarren. The fleet surged from port and began the hunt for the *Plagueclaw*, though they were to encounter something far, far worse. In the shadow of the Frenerax Dust Cloud, the fleet was ambushed by a force of Chaos warships led by the *Terminus Est*, flagship of the Herald of Nurgle, Typhus himself. The battle was short and bloody, with several Imperial ships crippled in the opening salvo of torpedoes, while others were overrun by vile, diseased creatures that vomited forth from loathsome boarding craft. Admiral Quarren recovered well and rallied his forces superbly, counterattacking and fighting his way clear of the trap. Typhus did not pursue and the majority of Quarren's fleet was able to limp back to port. The Battle of Frenerax had been a costly disaster, but there was worse to come.

During the return journey to Belis Corona, thousands of crewmen sickened and died and only with the help of system pilots was the fleet able to dock safely. But if the situation at Belis Corona was bad, it was worse elsewhere. Many of the plague hulks had slipped through the defensive net and the same contagion that had struck down the ships' crews was spreading like wildfire through many inhabited worlds in the Cadian and Agripinaa sectors as well as those of the Belis Corona sub sector. The Hive world of Subiaco Diablo proved to be an ideal breeding ground for the unknown plague and was quickly quarantined by officers from the Officio Medicae, but not before millions had already perished. Within a month, a dozen other worlds reported cases of the plague and panic spread as transit between neighbouring sectors was halted in an effort to stem further infection.

As the epedemic spread, apocalyptic sects began appearing on every world afflicted, preaching that the Emperor's wrath had descended upon them and was a punishment for their sins of wickedness and vice. Only the faithful would be spared the Curse of Unbelief and hordes of flagellating devotees filled the streets of every world around the Eye of Terror. The continued health of these fanatics gave their words the sheen of truth and millions flocked to hear their fiery rhetoric. The plague continued to spread, but it was on Subiaco Diablo that the true horror of the plague was finally revealed. To the shock and disgust of the the planet's inhabitants, the mass graves deep in the ash plains heaved and split, the corpses of those who had perished in the plague climbing from the lime-encrusted ground. Soon millions of shambling corpses were advancing on the hive, clawing their way inside and attacking the weakened inhabitants.

Within months, plague zombies were climbing from their graves on scores of worlds throughout the Belis Corona and Agripinaa sectors, and Imperial forces were stretched to the limit in containing these abominations as well as mobs of flagellating zealots who burned medicae ward facilities to the ground in their misguided attempts to halt the plague. Paralysed by the sheer scale of the epidemic, the Naval forces in these regions were completely unprepared for the vast Chaos fleet that emerged at the edge of the Subiaco Diablo system and surged into Imperial space. The Herald of Nurgle, the Traveller, Typhus of the Death Guard had come to reap the harvest of his plague, and nothing stood ready to stop him.

THE BLACK CRUSADES OF ABADDON THE DESPOILER

Abaddon the Despoiler, the Arch Heretic whose name is a curse on a thousand worlds, once led the First Company of the Luna Wolves, and was as devoted and brave a warrior as any. The Emperor later honoured Horus's Legion by decreeing that its name be changed to the Sons of Horus, but when the Heresy erupted, it was clear that Abaddon's loyalties lay with the Warmaster. Abaddon fought at the forefront of the war, zealously tearing asunder that which he had once helped conquer in the name of the Emperor. Abaddon was Horus's most favoured warrior and it was rumoured that he was in fact the Warmaster's clone son. When the final battle of the Heresy came, Abaddon was fighting on another part of the Warmaster's battle barge, though he felt the psychic shockwave of Horus's death resonate through the Warp and his scream of anguish plunged him deeper into madness than any mortal should ever fall. He fought his way to the bridge and found the corpse of his beloved Warmaster, taking the lightning claw from Horus's wrist for his own.

Though every instinct screamed at Abaddon to wreak his vengeance, he knew that the forces left to him were not enough to win the day. Horus's last gamble had failed and the war was over. Taking command of the battle barge, Abaddon led the retreat to the Eye of Terror, assuming command of the Sons of Horus and renaming them the Black Legion. Abaddon vanished into the Eye of Terror and entered the realms of dark legend. Decades passed before Abaddon was to return, surging from the Eye at the head of a massive army and smashing aside the defenders to pour forth into Imperial space. For a time, it looked as though Abaddon would succeed in breaking through the defences around the Eye of Terror, and only the combined might of several Space Marine Chapters and the Titan Legions finally halted this first of Abaddon's Black Crusades.

Since that day, there have been eleven separate Black Crusades, ranging from small raids to sector-spanning conflicts that have cost the lives of millions of Imperial soldiers. On the world of El'Phanor, the Despoiler exterminated the kin of the Kromarch and on Mackan, Abaddon earned the eternal hatred of the Blood Angels when he slew their warriors and violated their flesh. Beneath the Tower of Silence on Uralan, Abaddon was led to the daemon sword Drach'nyen by a golden-skinned stranger and with this cursed item, carved himself a realm of diabolical evil within the Eye of Terror before plunging the Gothic sector into war. Once more the Imperium was victorious, but the cost of victory was high and two of the Blackstone Fortress, powerful weapons created in ancient times by long-forgotten hands, were lost to the Despoiler. Numerous other incursions, too scattered and random to be called Black Crusades have plagued the Cadian Sector and there can be no respite while this most evil of heretics still lives.

Now, dire portents wax nigh and even the most blinkered cannot fail to see a pattern emerging in the attacks in the sectors surrounding the Eye of Terror. The Emperor's Tarot regularly displays powerful cards representing war and death on an apocalyptic scale, and Astropaths report horrifying visions of torrents of blood raining from the sky to drown the Imperium of Man. Even the Eldar, aloof and cruel aliens, have given warning of the rise of a Great Uniter, as deep within the anarchy of the Eye of Terror, ancient feuds have been set aside in the face of Abaddon's leadership. Bitter hatreds, such as that between the World Eaters and the Emperor's Children following the Battle of Skalathrax, have been quelled and even the Alpha Legion and the Word Bearers share an uneasy peace. Binding oaths and debts have been called to account and a force, the likes of which has not been seen since the Horus Heresy, has been assembled, ready to strike the Imperium like a thunderbolt.

THE WAR IN THE WEB

His heart was beating a rapid tattoo within his chest, and Niadien had to concentrate to contain his excitement. It was difficult to do so this close to the Avatar's throne room, and doubly so on the eve of battle, but it would not do to show such an unseemly display of emotion before his Farseer. Eldrad Ulthran had called him here to the Dome of Crystal Seers by name and, though he was intensely curious as to why, given that he was a warrior not a seer, he was impatient to return to his training. Niadien carried his helmet in the crook of his arm, the flexible wraithbone armour feeling natural against his body and the spirits of its former wearers filling him with the urge to fight. Dimly, he remembered the moment he had forsaken the life of Niadien the poet to become Niadien the Striking Scorpion Exarch, but that was a long time ago, and such thoughts were fleeting and ephemeral in the face of the prospect of battle against the forces of the ancient enemy. The wraithbone of the Craftworld pulsed with aggression and a thrumming current of barely suppressed violence saturated every Eldar with the lust for battle. The Avatar was close to waking and its dreams of violence and bloodshed permeated every facet of Ulthwé. The air sang with the promise of battle and Niadien felt its call resonate in every fibre of his being.

"The Bloody Handed One calls to you, does he not, Niadien?" said a soft voice behind him. He spun, hand involuntarily reaching for his sword, but relaxing as he saw the venerable Farseer. Eldrad Ulthran made his way awkwardly through the softly glowing crystal trees of the dome, leaning heavily on his ornately carved staff. Niadien saw that his flesh shone with a faint, crystalline light, the skin translucent and unyielding.

Niadien nodded curtly. "Yes, I can feel his heat burning in my veins. The call to war is one I cannot refuse."

"I know," said Eldrad softly. "It is your appointed path, and to deny that is to walk the road that has but one end."

Eldrad stopped beside a long and gracefully curved crystal tree, its structure veined with darting lights and the suggestion of a peaceful face swimming in its depths.

"These are dark times for our people, Niadien," began Eldrad. "The one called the Despoiler readies his armies and the Mon-Keigh do not heed my warnings."

"What has this to do with us, Lord Ulthran?" growled Niadien. "If the Mon-Keigh wish to destroy themselves, let them. Ulthwé is all that matters."

The Farseer nodded. "Normally I would agree with you, but there are other forces at work here, Niadien. The silver warriors of the Yngir have returned."

"The Necrontyr? After so long?"

"Yes. They seek to destroy the remaining Talismans of Vaul and without them, we are helpless against the star gods."

"We should have taken them from the Mon-Keigh before they could lose them to the Despoiler," said Niadien, unable to contain the venom in his tone.

"True," agreed Eldrad, "but the Jackal God's foresight stretches from the dawn of time and eclipses even mine. He isolated the Gothic sector and we had not the strength to stop him. But there is worse, Niadien. Ahriman, the sorcerer of the Red Cyclops, has breached the webway and he brings his soulless warriors and the power of ancient magicks."

Niadien recoiled in horror at the thought of a minion of Chaos within the sacred pathways of the Eldar. Such an affront could not be tolerated and his warrior's spirit burned with fury at this upstart Mon-Keigh's temerity.

"He seeks the Black Library and the ancient knowledge it contains. He must not discover it, for there are secrets it keeps that should never have been revealed, even to us."

"He will not discover it while I draw breath," assured Niadien. "My strike force is assembled and our webway portal is prepared. We await only your order to depart. Send us to war, Lord Ulthran!"

"In time, Niadien, in time," soothed Eldrad, staring wistfully at the crystal trees of his ancestors; Farseers stretching back to the time of the Fall. "The Dark Kin are also aware of the breach in the webway and mass for war. Their efforts to save the twilight city of Commorragh will be in vain and the bloodshed they will unleash will only make things worse. There is one amongst them who thirsts for my death and he does not care that his actions will lead his people, as well as ours, to their doom."

"What would you have me do, Lord Ulthran?"

Eldrad turned and rested his hand upon the shoulder guard of Niadien's armour, feeling the lust for violence of all the Exarchs who had worn the armour before Niadien straining to be unleashed in battle once more.

"We must awake the Avatar of Kaela Mensha Khaine, Niadien. We will need his strength and the fury of his presence to prevail in the coming war. I have seen many futures leading to this point and in all of them the Avatar walks among us."

Niadien felt his heart swell with pride as he realised what must come next.

"This is why I have called you here," said Eldrad mournfully, drawing a garland of wraithornes from a pouch at his waist.

"You have been chosen, Niadien. You are to be the Young King."

THE THIRTEENTH CRUSADE OF ABADDON THE DESPOILER

As the plague known as the Curse of Unbelief swept through many Imperial worlds throughout the Belis Corona and Agripinaa sectors, cults preaching that the Imperium had forsaken the teachings of the Emperor grew in numbers. Decrying the sufferers' sickness as just punishment for their wickedness, they claimed that only in the flames and purgation of pain could the cure be found, and they would provide both. On Malin's Reach and Lelithar, Imperial rule all but broke down as the plague crippled the authorities' ability to contain the zealots and screaming demagogues who whipped the mobs into a frenzy of destruction and self-mutilation. Naval facilities and symbols of Imperial rule were openly attacked and over the following weeks, mob rule virtually replaced that of the Administratum on many outlying worlds.

Such vast outpourings of zeal and bloodshed echoed in the Warp, stirring the already volatile Immaterium into new and violent life. The fringes of Warp Storm Baphomael expanded to engulf the edges of the Cadian system and Astropaths based at Kasr Partox reported terrible visions depicting vast plains of mutilated bodies and worlds burned with fire. Such incidences grew and spread throughout the sector until it was to manifest in a horrifying manner on the world of Belisar in the Choir Chamber of Astropaths, high on the spire of Hive Teriax. During a routine auto-séance, the senior Adept of Astropaths began convulsing, his flesh blazing with psychic energy. Emergency warp-dampers and null shields dropped into place, but it was already too late as uncontrollable energies burst through into the material world and the top nine levels of the hive spire were instantly vaporised in a massive psychic explosion.

The signs were unmistakable and everything pointed towards a calamity of terrifying proportions. Readings of the Emperor's Tarot produced dire portents, and omens of a fearful nature began appearing across the Segmentum. Many of these proved to be false, but rumour and hearsay passed into fact, and fear and paranoia whipped entire populations into terrified, panicked hysteria. Members of the Frateris Clergy, Confessors, Preachers and Cardinals, were despatched from the Synod Ministra on Ophelia VII to provide calm, spiritual and authoritative guidance, but such was the widespread panic that their voices went largely unheard. Amidst the fear that gripped Imperial

citizens, almost lost among all the other incidences of terror and bloodshed, unknown raiders attacked the outlying Agri-world of Dentor. The crew of a bulk freighter delivering agricultural machinery discovered this atrocity, finding entire communities butchered like livestock and the landscape burned. Nothing was taken and no motive could be ascertained. No more could be done and the report was buried under the more pressing matters that continued to prey upon Segmentum authorities.

On Cadia itself, the Adepts tasked with the study of the ancient pylons became aware of a new and unsettling development. The pylons, which had until now been utterly inert, began resonating with an almost imperceptible vibration. Research teams were immediately despatched to investigate and their findings were disturbing to say the least. Microscopic stress fractures were developing along the previously impenetrable surfaces of the pylons and all were resonating at an amplitude similar to that produced by a Gellar Field, the invisible energy field that shields a starship travelling through the Warp. The pylons appeared to be fighting to hold back the power of warp storm Baphomael, but were, slowly but surely, destroying themselves in the process.

Disintegration

Yet more reports of brutal raids filtered back to Segmentum command, echoing the savagery of the attack on Dentor. Isolated settlements in the Sarlax and Amistel systems fell to the mysterious raiders, with each attack more vicious and bloodthirsty than the last. Naval patrols attempted to police the space around the eastern reaches of the Agripinaa sector, but their resources were stretched thinly as it was.

Following yet another raid, this time against an Imperial research facility on Malin's Reach, the 31st Destroyer Squadron (Deathbringers) operating out of Demios Binary was attacked and destroyed by unknown ambushers.

External pict-capture recovered by salvage teams recorded confused images of what appeared to be twisted and perverted variants of Space Marine vessels attacking the Cobra class destroyers, and internal logs, though fragmentary, showed boarders in blue and gold armour butchering the crew. As the attacks continued, the Navy pulled all its ships back to port and Tactical Strategos identified a pattern in the attacks that appeared to be moving inexorably inwards from the eastern sub sectors and directly towards Cadia.

As Naval forces in the Agripinaa sector retreated to their bases, yet more disaster was to befall the beleaguered Imperial forces. On Lelithar, a powerful figure arose amongst the raving cults and fanatics, proclaiming himself the Voice of the Emperor. An orator of fearsome skill, this mysterious individual roused entire populations with his passionate speeches and screaming fanatics overran those facilities that remained in Imperial hands, such as spaceports and fortified military bases. Scores of ships and entire arsenals of weaponry were seized as the followers of the Voice took to the stars. His emissaries spread throughout the sector, and cults of the Voice emerged on Yayor, Amistel, Albitern and even amongst the inmates of the prison world of Bar-el. As destructive as the Cults of the Voice were, they spurred a battered Imperium into life, preachers and missionaries of the Missionarus Galaxia spreading through the affected regions and decrying the evil of the anti Imperial cult. Imperial faith rose like a phoenix from the flames and furious battles erupted between the followers of the Voice and pious servants of the Emperor. Far from destroying the faith of these sectors, there was a resurgence of vows of piety. Imperial assassins and kill-teams were despatched to terminate the leader of this cult, though none were ever seen again. Only one garbled communication, from a lone Vindicare Assassin, gives a clue to identity of the Voice of the Emperor; a hooded figure carrying a sword and a pair of exquisite pistols.

Betrayal on Cadia

Despite disintegrating Imperial rule throughout the sectors surrounding the Eye of Terror, Cadia remained a disciplined centre of control. To combat the increasing frequency and scale of Chaos activities, the military high command ordered that every Shock Troop regiment muster on Cadia. Hundreds of extra landing fields were constructed at Kasr Tyrok and the infrastructure required to support such a muster gathered from Kasr Holn, Helotas and Fremas. Millions of soldiers had already been assembled when the Volscani regiment, considered by many to be the most hardened fighters in the sector, landed on Cadia. Vast dropships brought Leviathan command transports onto Cadian soil and as the high command prepared to receive the salute of the newly arrived regiment, the Volscani revealed their true colours. Banners bearing blasphemous Chaos icons unfurled from the building-sized transports and their massive guns opened fire, destroying the command Leviathan of Governor Primus, Marus Porelska. Volscani troops poured onto the landing fields and attacked the awaiting Cadians, falling on them with unbridled savagery and killing with the ferocity and discipline they were famed for.

Battle raged around the spaceport for over an hour, but with so many defenders in place, there could be only one outcome. The Volscani were defeated, but at terrible cost. The Governor Primus and most of the ranking officers were dead and what was left of the Cadian command structure struggled to maintain order. As the last scattered pockets of resistance were hunted down, the Lord Castellan, Ursarkar Creed, took over the reeling Cadian forces, quickly restoring a measure of command and control following the atrocity. As Ursarkar Creed fought on the bloody fields of Kasr Tyrok, the most trusted advisor to the Governor Secundus collapsed deep inside the fortress of Kasr Vazan, his body bloating and rotting in a manner all too familiar to the chirurgeons of the Cadian Sector. The Kasrkin reacted with admirable speed, but it was too late for the troopers of Kasr Vazan and within an hour, the entire fortress was declared Unclean and sealed forever.

The Calm before the Storm
There could be no doubt now that a major incursion from the Eye of Terror was imminent, and the newly-instated Governor Primus, Ursarkar Creed, ordered the Cadian forces to dig in, strengthening their defences, stockpiling munitions, war materiel and food and water. Hurried pleas for aid from forces beyond the Cadian Sector were despatched with the highest authentication codes and within days, missives from the Space Wolves and a number of other Chapters of Space Marines arrived, pledging warriors and naval assets to join the fight. Regimental musters were begun in scores of nearby sectors as the Administratum reacted to the threat with a haste unheard of in such a monolithic organisation. Imperial forces were gathering, but it would be many weeks, if not months before enough strength could be gathered. In addition, an unconfirmed report of a fortress monastery afloat on a massive bedrock was filed by Captain Urquarn of the Gothic class cruiser, *Abridal's Glory*, but many of the ship's crew were suffering from fatigue from long tours of duty and his report was dismissed as the hallucinations of an over-tired crew.

In addition to this, Cobra squadrons patrolling the edges of the Eye of Terror filed numerous sightings of Eldar ships, though the Navy was unable to engage the aliens, as their speed soon carried them beyond weapons' range. Fleet command was at first alarmed by these reports, but the Eldar ships seemed more concerned with flight than combat and there were no reported engagements between the two forces. Hurried investigations of the worlds the Eldar were abandoning revealed them to be unusually verdant, with strange, xeno constructions that Astropaths divined to be warp gates that had been recently, and permanently, sealed. Why the Eldar would abandon these worlds and seal off their precious warp gates was just one mystery amongst hundreds that had surfaced in the preceding months and there were not the resources to investigate fully.

As the Cadian forces prepared for the inevitable attack, yet more assaults from the unknown raiders hit the Tabor and Ulthor systems, but this time vessels of the Imperial Navy were in position to counterattack. Three squadrons of Cobra Destroyers in conjunction with the Lunar class cruiser, *Goliath*, pursued the attackers into the Faberius Straits and in a fearsome battle, crippled the Styx class cruiser, *Darkblood*. The engagement cost the Navy most of the Cobras and the *Goliath* was severely damaged, but at last the attackers had been identified. The *Darkblood* was codified as being attached to the Night Lords warleader, Tarraq Darkblood, one of the most vicious killers in a Legion replete with sadistic butchers. Before Imperial reinforcements could arrive, a huge force of Chaos warships were picked up on long-range augers, and the surviving Imperial vessels were forced to withdraw, limping to the safety of the nearby port of Aurent.

The Storm Breaks
As part of the constant vigil around the Eye of Terror, highly trained units of Kasrkin were pushed into the swirling maelstrom, desperate to find some indication of where the first blow would land. Astropathic divination pointed towards the blighted world of Urthwart, where a massive force was believed to be gathering. Urthwart was a world taken by Chaos, its population enslaved and sacrificed to the dark gods. The Kasrkin found nothing alive on Urthwart, merely death and hideous plague zombies infected with the Curse of Unbelief. But as the Kasrkin prepared to withdraw, frantic vox communication from their ships in orbit reported numerous vessels advancing on Urthwart from the Eye of Terror. The Kasrkin fell back to their dropships and attempted to return to their carriers, but it was already too late. The Imperial ships were either crippled or had been forced to disengage and make for Cadia. There was to be no escape and the Cadians were stranded on Urthwart as a massive vessel, larger than the most gargantuan capital ship approached them: the Planet Killer.

Oblivious to their fate, the Cadians could do nothing as the incomprehensible power of the Planet Killer was unleashed in a devastating lance of energy that bored through the planet's crust and sundered the very bedrock. The land split and the planet's core exploded, breaking Urthwart into spinning pieces of molten rock. The death of Urthwart echoed in the Warp, blowing out the encroaching warp storms, and every telepath within a thousand light years felt its death scream. As Urthwart collapsed in on itself, a Chaos fleet of hundreds of warships and hulking transports surged from the depths of the Eye of Terror towards Cadia. The diseased *Plagueclaw* and *Terminus Est*, along with a massive flotilla of plague hulks, emerged in the Subiaco Diablo system and began heading deep into the pestilence-wracked sector. Alongside the Chaos fleet, and guarded by the Despoiler class battleships *Merciless Death* and *Fortress of Agony*, came two hideously altered Blackstone Fortresses. Where once they had served the Imperium as Naval bases, they now resembled twisted and mutated cathedrals, dedicated only to blood and death.

Naval patrols, forewarned by the surviving Astropaths on Belisar, fell back before the tide of corrupted vessels, desperately calling for aid from neighbouring sectors. The ban on transit between sectors was still in force and precious hours were wasted as Naval captains fought to overcome the bureaucracy of the Officio Medicae who attempted to prevent them from press-ganging their crews back into service. Those ships that could be mustered gathered in the Ormantep system under the command of Admiral Pulaski, ready to fight and die to give the defenders on Cadia whatever time they could buy with their lives. Unlike many other naval battles, there was no jockeying for advantageous position by the foes. The Chaos fleet obviously intended to batter its way through the Imperial Navy and the two fleets clashed in the shadow of the Ilthirium Belt, a mineral rich asteroid field plundered by the mining hulks of Ormantep.

Battle was joined and the horrendously outnumbered loyalist fleet fought in the grand tradition of the Imperial Navy, with courage, honour and steadfastness. A dozen vessels were crippled in the opening moments of the battle, either by wave after wave of torpedoes or constant attack runs of Doomfire bombers, but the rest of the fleet fought on. As both fleets intermingled and the battle became a desperate, close quarters engagement, with horrific damage being inflicted on both sides, a portion of the Chaos fleet split from the main battle and surged past the heavily engaged Navy towards the Agripinaa sector. For long hours the two fleets pounded one another, and all hope seemed lost when Admiral Pulaski's flagship, *Honour and Duty*, was destroyed in a catastrophic plasma drive explosion. The Imperial defenders had commended their souls to the Emperor when several Chaos warships that had assumed blocking positions suddenly exploded as the warships of Battlefleet Agripinaa caught the Chaos fleet off guard. Led by Admiral Quarren, the newly arrived Imperial reinforcements cleared a path for the beleaguered Navy to disengage from the battle and withdraw to Demios Binary.

Quarren had saved what remained of the fleet, but in doing so had left the way clear for the splinter fleet of Chaos vessels to breach the defences of the Agripinaa sector. With little or nothing to prevent the Chaos ships from entering each planet's orbit, the systems of the Agripinaa sector were wide open to attack by the diseased followers of the Plague God. Soon the worlds of this and the Belis Corona sub sector became nightmare visions of hell, mud, horror and war. On Amistel Majoris, cursed Plague Marines of Nurgle landed and decimated much of the local defence forces before the forces of the Drookian Fen Guard were able to effect planetfall and bolster the embattled defenders. Plague took many hundreds of lives and the once verdant fields of this prosperous world were reduced to desolate, corpse choked plains, with bodies piled ten deep in every crater. Colonel Pertaj orchestrated a masterful defence, devising a cunning series of trench systems to confound the foe and lead them into deadly fire traps. But the colonel never lived to see his defences in action as the plague struck him down before the first major engagement of the war. Space Marines from the Howling Griffons Chapter fought their way through the Chaos blockade, escorting the ships of the Legio Astorum, to man the defences as the first wave of attackers struck. Only the Space Marines, with their blessed power armour and Titans could survive the toxin-ridden battlefields of this plague front and the normally lightning fast warfare practiced by the warriors of the Adeptus Astartes bogged down into gruelling trench fighting. Both sides fed their forces into the meat grinder of battle, neither willing to surrender the world to the other.

On Lelithar, the originating world of the Voice, Imperial Guard soldiers of the Jouran Dragoons, together with Warlord Titans of the Legio Ignatum landed at Gorgosa and laid siege to the captured Imperial palace, said to be the operational headquarters of the Voice. The resultant siege decimated much of Lelithar's capital city and cost the lives of millions of people as the city's populace rose to fight the soldiers of the Imperial Guard. Supported by the Death Spectres Chapter, the siege continues to grind mercilessly towards an uncertain conclusion.

Plague swept across the face of every world and as many soldiers fell to disease as to the weapons of the enemy. In space, Admiral Quarren led the battered fleet in a fighting retreat back to Cadia and stationed it in a defensive posture in conjunction with the three Ramilies class star forts in orbit. The Chaos fleet advanced towards Cadia, stopping only to allow the Blackstone Fortresses to scour Demios Binary to a barren rock. Lightning arcs of incandescent energies razed the planet's surface bare, killing millions of Imperial servants and destroying every structure in a matter of hours. Chaos vessels quickly overwhelmed the orbital defences of Solar Mariatus, the outermost planet of the Cadian system, and hundreds of dropships carrying traitor regiments of Volscani Cataphracts descended to the surface, attacking the mining outposts and capturing the valuable ore refineries from the defending units of the Cadian 23rd.

Here, the traitor forces established a forward base of operations from which to launch attacks throughout the system. St. Josmane's Hope fell soon after, the inmates of this military prison rising up against their gaolers as the first waves of the Violators renegade Space Marines attacked. Brutal, close-quarters fighting erupted all across the continent-sized prison and many of the guards kept a bullet for themselves rather than be taken by the frenzied inmates. Welcoming the traitor forces as liberators, the inmates were to be horrifyingly disabused of this notion as those allowed to live were instead taken as slaves for the Chaos fleet or conscripted into its armies. Enemy ships spread throughout the Cadian system, several being picked off by shadowy Eldar vessels that vanished as mysteriously as they arrived, but the bulk of the Chaos fleet advanced directly on Cadia.

Admiral Quarren had done what he could, but the overwhelming Chaos fleet could not be stopped and after three days of hard fighting, the majority of his ships had been either crippled or destroyed. Those vessels that could escape fled to the Forge world of Kantrael in an attempt to refit and rearm in time to make a difference, but there were precious few of them. A single Ramilies star fort fell to the invaders, the remaining two managing to overload their reactors and self-destruct before the enemy could consolidate their hold upon them. With the space around Cadia secured, orbital bombardments hammered the planet's surface and, one by one, the defence batteries were silenced. Hundreds of cargo hulks moved into orbit and disgorged swarms of landing craft that streaked through the planet's upper atmosphere.

The invasion of Cadia had begun.

To: Lord Inquisitor Goreden,
       Ordo Xenos, Nemesis Tessera
From: Interrogator Kieras, Clearance Omicron
Subject : Ahriman of the Thousand Sons
Priority: Ultra High, immediate action requested.

Received: 999.M41
Message Format: Telepathic
Astropathic Duct: Chima Lomas
Thought for the Day: Wisdom is the
                          beginning of fear.

Honoured inquisitor, allow me to introduce myself to you. My name is Ferdan Kieras, a loyal servant of the God-Emperor and former pupil of Inquisitor Czevak. It has been both my pleasure and honour to serve the honourable Inquisitor for nearly five decades in an investigative capacity, seeking out information as well as undertaking other, more esoteric missions involving xeno creatures. As sign of my truth, I urge you to seek counsel from the Biologis at Nemesis Tessera and verify the gene sequence data attached to this message. But now to the substance of this missive.

It is with heavy heart I bring to your attention the disappearance of my master. I fear a terrible fate has befallen him, and it was his instruction that in such circumstances, I should contact you and seek guidance. It had long been a dread to my master that the being known as Ahriman of the Thousand Sons discover his whereabouts and force him to reveal hidden knowledge imparted to him by the Eldar. To fully understand the dire implications of this, I must unfortunately reveal to you much knowledge that should best remain secret.

As I am sure you are aware, Ahriman was once a Librarian in the Thousand Sons Legion of Space Marines, and under the tutelage of his Primarch, Magnus the Red, learned much of the ways of sorcery. In time his mastery of blasphemous magicks was almost the equal of his cyclopean Primarch and his knowledge of forbidden lore corrupted him beyond redemption. The Thousand Sons were also tainted and Ahriman realised that the Legion would soon be reduced to little more than gibbering monstrosities. He conceived a great spell to save the Legion, called the Rubric of Ahriman. Its energies were more powerful than he could possibly have anticipated and its effects on the Thousand Sons devastating. Only those with sorcererous powers were spared its effect, while the remainder of the Legion were reduced to dust within their sealed suits of armour, becoming little more than fighting automatons. Enraged with Ahriman's betrayal, Magnus cast him out and since that day, Ahriman has sought ever more powerful artefacts to increase his understanding of the Warp.

One source of lore that has always eluded him is the Black Library, a vast repository of ancient secrets collated by the Eldar and gathered together in a hidden place, unknown to the eyes of Man. Only those pure of heart and with the strength of mind to comprehend the scale of such awful knowledge may enter this place and sup from its wisdom, and my master was one such individual. Ahriman has long sought Inquisitor Czevak in order to wrest the location of the Black Library from his mind, but through cunning and machination, my master has thus far eluded his nemesis. But recent developments lead me to believe that the dread sorcerer has finally caught up with him. A Savant in my employ, having accessed secret files of the Ordo Malleus regarding Ahriman, was recently found dead, and psychometric readings revealed an individual who could be none other than Ahriman himself as his killer. A number of other incidents, at first glance unconnected, but upon further scrutiny linked in the subtlest of ways, all point to the same dire conclusion. My master's last contact was in the region of space known as the Sentinel worlds and it is here that I shall begin my search. I shall investigate further, but it seems clear to me that Ahriman of the Thousand Sons has ensnared Inquisitor Czevak.

If this proves to be the case, then I urge you to use whatever power you can bring to bear on this matter and despatch all force that can be gathered to hunt down this heretic sorcerer and stop him before he achieves whatever nefarious plan he intends to implement.

Yours in desperate need,

Kieras

Interrogator Kieras.

Sweet merciful Emperor, the secrets of the Black Library unlocked by the sorcerer of the Red Cyclops! Better that Czevak has perished to some foul xeno creature than fall into his clutches. I shall mobilise the 34th Gudrunite Rifles and petition the Chapter Master of the Iron Hands for his warriors' aid.

I pray I am not too late.

FORCE DISPOSITIONS AT THE OUTSET OF THE THIRTEENTH BLACK CRUSADE OF ABADDON THE DESPOILER

COMPILER'S NOTE: Due to the sheer scope of the theatre of operations in which the forces listed below operated, these figures should be considered little more than conjecture. The status of the forces of the Imperium changed rapidly during the initial stages of the conflict, and no true record of their disposition could be made. Later in the conflict, reinforcements flooded in from the entire region, and Cadian Sector Command lost all track of the number and status of the units involved. Furthermore, those figures relating to the forces of the Despoiler were based on unreliable and rapidly changing intelligence, the nature of which was virtually impossible for any sane man to decipher.

The Blessed Forces of the God-Emperor of Mankind

KNOWN LEGIONNES ASTARTES

ANGELS OF ABSOLUTION	10 Companies
ANGELS OF VIGILANCE	5 Companies
ANGELS SANGUINE	7 Companies
BRAZEN CLAWS	10 Companies
DARK ANGELS	10 Companies
DEATH SPECTRES	6 Companies
DOOM EAGLES	5 Companies
EXORCISTS	10 Companies
EXCORIATORS*	8 Companies
HARBINGERS	8 Companies
HOWLING GRIFFONS	8 Companies
IRON HANDS	10 Clans
IRON KNIGHTS	1 Company
IRON SNAKES	5 Companies
MARINES EXEMPLAR*	9 Companies
NIGHT WATCH*	11 Companies
NOVAMARINES	6 Companies
RELICTORS*	10 Companies
SUBJUGATORS*	3 Companies
SPACE WOLVES	12 Great Companies
STORM WARRIORS	10 Companies
ULTRAMARINES	1 Honour Company
WHITE CONSULS*	10 Companies

++CONTINUED IN FILE QW/77++

* The Mythos Angelica Mortis makes reference to a group of twenty Chapters known as the Astartes Praeses. The tome claims that these chapters were founded with the express purpose of guarding the regions surrounding the Eye of Terror, although the identity and status of each individual chapter is not currently known.

RECORDED ADEPTA SORORITAS

GREATER ORDERS:

ORDER OF THE BLOODY ROSE	6 Preceptories
ORDER OF THE EBON CHALICE	4 Preceptories
ORDER OF OUR MARTYRED LADY	5 Preceptories

LESSER ORDERS:

ORDER OF THE ERMINE MANTLE	3 Missions
ORDER OF THE WOUNDED HEART	1 Commandery

NOTABLE IMPERIAL GUARD UNITS

AVELLORNIAN GUNNERS	32 Squadrons
BAR-EL PENAL LEGIONS	4 Legions
CADIAN KASRKIN	486 Companies
CADIAN SHOCK TROOPS	612 Regiments
CADIAN YOUTH ARMY	16 Regional Commands
DROOKIAN FEN GUARD	16 Companies
FINREHT HIGHLANDERS	3 Regiments
GUDRUNITE RIFLES	47 Regiments
JOURAN DRAGOONS	7 Regiments
KELLERSBURG IRREGULARS	3 Regiments
KNOVIAN GHARKAS	14 Regiments
MORDANT 303RD 'ACID DOGS'	1 Regiment
NARSINE YEOMANRY	32 Battle Groups
NECROMUNDAN 8TH 'THE SPIDERS'	1 Regiment
THRACIAN GUARD	35 Regiments
VAN DE'MANS WORLD 'REDBACKS'	5 Regiments
ZENONIAN FREE COMPANIES	9 Companies

++CONTINUED IN FILE NI/24++

ORDO MALLEUS

INQUISITORIAL TASK FORCES	CLASSIFIED
GREY KNIGHTS	CLASSIFIED
INQUISITORIAL STORMTROOPERS	
Nemesis Tessera	est. 38 Companies
Ocularis Terribus Warzone	CLASSIFIED

DEPARTMENTO MUNITORUM

ENGINEER CORPS	18
SEIGE AUXILIA CORPS	28 Counter-siege batteries

OFFICIO ASSASSINORUM

AGENTS	CLASSIFIED

TEMPLARS PSYKOLOGIS

DISRUPTION SQUADS	37
AUGUR TEAMS	6

NOTABLE ADEPTUS MECHANICUS

CENTURIO ORDINATUS	4 Ordinatus
HOUSE KRAST	2 Households
HOUSE AROKON	4 Households
LEGIO METALICA	Demi-Legio
LEGIO IGNATUM	Legio
LEGIO GRYPHONICUS	Legio
LEGIO ASTORUM	Legio
ORDO REDUCTOR	Demi-Legio
SKITARII	87 Regiments
DIVISIO TELEPATHICA PSI-TITANS	Classified

++CONTINUED IN FILE VX/99

IMPERIAL FLEET

+Vessels of Note

DUKE LURSTOPHAN	Dauntless class cruiser
ABRIDAL'S GLORY	Gothic class cruiser
HONOUR AND DUTY	Emperor class battleship

+Battlefleets of Note

BATTLEFLEET CADIA	12 Battleships
	12 Cruiser Squadrons
	21 Escort Squadrons
BATTLEFLEET CORONA	7 Battleships
	13 Cruiser Squadrons
	17 Escort Squadrons
BATTLEFLEET SCARUS	5 Battleships
	9 Cruiser Squadrons
	13 Escort Squadrons

+Estimated Total Fleet Assets

FRONT LINE BATTLE GROUPS	21
REAR ECHELON BATTLE GROUPS	36
INDEPENDENT STRIKE GROUPS	4
SPACE MARINE BATTLEBARGES	est. 21+
SPACE MARINE STRIKE CRUISERS	est. 150+
SPACE MARINE ESCORT SQUADRONS	est. 200+

++CONTINUED IN FILE HG/87++

See file ET/778/K2230z for summary of battle honours.
See files ET/340/Q1349-639 for estimated casualty figures.

The Forces of Abaddon the Despoiler

RECORDED TRAITOR LEGIONNES ASTARTES

ALPHA LEGION	20+ unconfirmed sightings-all sectors
BLACK LEGION	Major presence-all sectors
DEATH GUARD	Major presence-Subiaco Diablo
EMPEROR'S CHILDREN	Unconfirmed actions against Eldar reported
IRON WARRIORS	Suspected presence-Cadian system
NIGHT LORDS	Unconfirmed reports-all sectors
SONS OF MALICE	Active-Scelus sector
THOUSAND SONS	Active-Caliban and Prospero sectors
VIOLATORS	3 confirmed actions-Scelus sector
WARP GHOSTS	Unconfirmed sighting-Agripinaa system
WORLD EATERS	Significant involvement-all sectors
WORD BEARERS	Active-rear echelon sectors

KNOWN TRAITOR LEGIO TITANICUS

DEATHS HEADS	Major presence confirmed-Cadia
DEATH STALKERS	Unconfirmed involvement-Cadia
FIRE MASTERS	Limited presence-Cadian sector
IRON SKULLS	Major force sighted-Vorga Torq
LEGIO VULCANUM I	4 unconfirmed assaults-Belisar and Kromat
LEGIO VULCANUM II	Suspected presence-Subiaco Diablo

MAJOR TRAITOR GUARD UNITS

5TH COLUMNUS	Presence confirmed-Belis Corona
666TH REGIMENT OF FOOT	Confirmed presence-Cadia
DISCILIAN APOSTATES	Unconfirmed
JENEN IRONCLADS	Major presence-Kromat system
SENTREK FREEMEN	3 suspected sightings-Barisa system
THE TRAITOR 9TH	Significant presence-Kantrael system
UBRIDIUS LIGHT INFANTRY	Major presence-Cadian sector
VOLSCANI CATAPHRACTS	Active-Cadia

++CONTINUED IN FILE IO/57++

ESTIMATED MUTANT HORDES

THE ANNOINTED OF AQ'SI	6 attacks confirmed-Belisar system
THE SHYIS'SLAA	Linked to cult uprisings-Albitern system
THE STIGMATUS COVENANT	Significant presence-Mackan system
THE UNSANCTIFIED	Unconfirmed involvement-Bar-el system

++CONTINUED IN FILE DE/80

RECORDED TRAITOR FLEET UNITS

+Estimated Traitor Fleet Assets

BATTLE FLEETS	est. 38
BLACKSTONE FORTRESSES	2
'WOLF PACK' SQUADRONS	est 19

+Battlefleets of Note

THE GRAND FLEET OF THE DESPOILER

	7 Battleships
	13 heavy cruisers
	est. 23 cruiser squadrons
	est. 30 escort squadrons

THE FLEET OF KOSOLAX THE FORESWORN

	1 Battleship
	3 cruiser squadrons
	8 escort squadrons

THE PLAGUE FLEET OF TYPHUS, HERALD OF NURGLE

	Terminus Est
	2 Battleships
	3 heavy cruisers
	5 cruiser squadrons
	est. 12 escort squadrons

+Vessels of Note

PLAGUECLAW	Unknown class
DARKBLOOD	Styx class heavy cruiser
PLANET KILLER	Undesignated class capital vessel
MERCILESS DEATH	Despoiler class battleship
FORTRESS OF AGONY	Despoiler class battleship

++CONTINUED IN FILE WW/33++

...file ref. ET/398/X9344w... ...ref. Force dispositions... ...Ocularis Terribus warzone...
There is only the Emperor, and he is our shield and protector.

COLLECTING A CAMPAIGN FORCE

The Eye of Terror campaign is a vast conflict involving countless armies. To participate you can simply use your existing army or, if you are more ambitious, collect a new army complete with a background history that fits with the campaign.

You can field your existing army in the campaign, after all you know its strengths and weaknesses. However, you may want to tailor your force to the missions, using your squad of Veteran Space Marines instead of Terminators, for example. How about taking a look at the new Cadian army list in this book and adding a Youth Army squad to your force? Perhaps you've always wanted a Defiler in an already mobile Chaos army. It's fun inventing campaign badges to apply to all your vehicles, or a specific flag for your army standard bearer.

With the Eye of Terror campaign you've got a great opportunity to collect a second army, one that is at the very centre of the action. These forces are unique. For instance, the Cadian Shock Troops army features both elite troops and cadets. The Lost and the Damned horde is a Chaos army without Chaos Space Marines, giving modellers free reign to create the most unusual conversions.

New armies such as the Space Wolves 13th Company have troops that offer modellers a distinct new look: loyal warriors of the Imperium with armour that is marked by Chaos. Others, such as the Ulthwé Strike Force, have a strong theme running through the whole army, both in troops choice and overall paint scheme.

Remember, it's always a good idea when choosing a new army to begin with the Standard Missions Force Organisation chart shown below. You must have at least one HQ and two Troops units to start an army.

STANDARD MISSIONS

COMPULSORY	OPTIONAL
1 HQ	1 HQ
2 Troops	4 Troops
	3 Elites
	3 Fast Attack
	3 Heavy Support

HQ — ELITES

TROOPS — TROOPS — FAST ATTACK — HEAVY SUPPORT

A Youth Army squad has been added to this Cadian army.

ELITES — TROOPS — HEAVY SUPPORT — TROOPS

FAST ATTACK — HQ

A horde of the Lost and the Damned.

SPACE WOLVES 13TH COMPANY

Lost in the Eye of Terror for ten millennia, the Space Wolves 13th Company wear pre-Heresy Space Wolves colours. During countless centuries separated from their homeworld, these mighty warriors have been forced to repair battle damage with armour torn from the bodies of their fallen foes.

Tearing their enemies apart with razor-sharp talons, the fearless Wulfen are terrifying foes even to the battle-hardened minions of Chaos.

Sweeping down from the trees come the feral Space Wolves 13th Company.

Equal in skill to an elite Wolf Guard, the Storm Claws are battle-honed in the art of close combat. They are single-minded in their purpose: the destruction of the enemies of the divine Emperor.

Rune Priest

Storm Claws biker

PAINTING THE 13TH COMPANY

⦿ A layer of Codex Grey was applied over a black undercoat, leaving the colour in the recesses visible.

⦾ The edges of the armour were painted Fortress Grey.

- 19 -

LOYAL SPACE MARINE CHAPTERS

A selection of the Chapters fighting to uphold the honour of the Emperor of Mankind.

Ultramarines

Wolf Lord Logan Grimnar

Cunning and resourceful, the Old Wolf's thirst for battle will only be quenched by the slaughter of the forces of Chaos.

Dark Angels

Iron Hands

Doom Eagles

Revilers

Angels Sanguine

White Consuls

Howling Griffons

The Space Wolves seek to purge the battlefield of the plague-ridden Death Guard and Defiler.

CHAOS SPACE MARINE LEGIONS

The legions of Chaos who seek to set the universe alight with unquenchable fires of Chaos.

Black Legion

Iron Warriors

Abaddon the Despoiler

Leading his dreaded Black Legion, Abaddon has won the favour of the Chaos gods. None can stand before his might.

World Eaters

Violators

Alpha Legion

Word Bearers

Thousand Sons

Emperor's Children

THE LOST AND THE DAMNED

Who knows what form the horrifying hordes of Chaos will take? The never-ending tide of mutants and the very spawn of Chaos seek to consume all before them. Not only this but the defenders of Mankind face their own kin turned traitor, the mightiest of all being the brutal Chaos Space Marines.

Whole armies of Imperial Guardsmen turn traitor and use treachery as well as their battle skills to destroy the chosen of the Emperor.

The foulest blessings of Chaos are most richly bestowed on the hordes of Mutants.

Like a grim tide of unholy horror and death come the hordes of the Lost and the Damned.

- The uniform was painted a base colour of Chaos Black.
- This was highlighted with an equal parts mix of Chaos Black and Bleached Bone.
- The detail was painted Scab Red.

Most favoured of all the Legions of the Damned, the Chaos Space Marines and monstrous Defilers shed the blood of the righteous in an eternal sacrifice of skulls and souls.

EYE OF TERROR

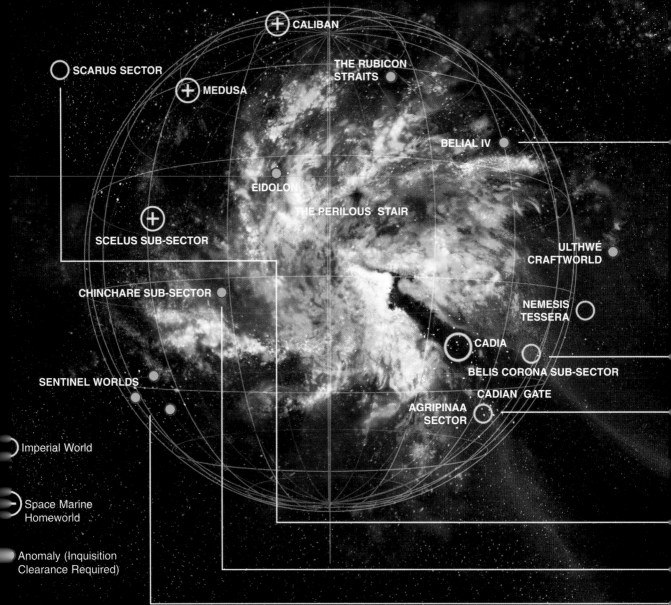

CALIBAN

SCARUS SECTOR

THE RUBICON STRAITS

MEDUSA

BELIAL IV

EIDOLON

THE PERILOUS STAIR

SCELUS SUB-SECTOR

ULTHWÉ CRAFTWORLD

CHINCHARE SUB-SECTOR

NEMESIS TESSERA

CADIA

SENTINEL WORLDS

BELIS CORONA SUB-SECTOR

CADIAN GATE

AGRIPINAA SECTOR

Imperial World

Space Marine Homeworld

Anomaly (Inquisition Clearance Required)

Cadia is a fortress world, the guardian of the one stable route from the Eye of Terror. Its entire population is geared for war and its factories and manufactorum churn out munitions, weapons and tanks at a prodigious rate. It is perhaps the most vital location in the entire Imperium and the military strength based there is unfeasibly vast. 71.75% of its population are under arms. Largest exporter of arms and munitions in region.

CADIA SYSTEMS

Kasr Sonnen - Fortress world

Kasr Partox - Fortress world

Korolis - Promethian weapons grade atomic materials produced here

St. Josmane's Hope - Military prison

Prosan - Hostile environment training ground

Solar Mariatus - source of much war materiel

Vigilatum - Naval training world

Macharia - Militarised hive world

Kasr Holn - Fortress world

Cadia - Lynchpin fortress world of sector

CADIA

C1.0.17
Orb. Dist. 1.32 AU
1.12G/Temp 20°C
Fortress /
Garrison World
Tithe Grade:
Adeptus Non
Aestimare: A3
Population:
250,000,000

BELIAL IV

One of the early Eldar homeworlds, Belial was pulled towards the Eye of Terror during the Fall and is now known as a Crone world, deserted and abandoned. It is home to a sacred Eldar artefact of black crystal, a sword forged from the energies of death.

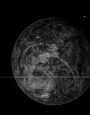

OX345.44
Orb. Dist. 6.67
0.97G/Temp 11
Xeno World
Tithe Grade: Adeptus Non
Aestimare: Z666
Population: No indigenous
lifeforms recorded

BEL

With a
Contai
additi

BELIS CORONA

A vast conglomeration of orbital dockyards, the naval facility orbits the dead world of Belis Corona. Entire battlefleets can be serviced here and the munitions stockpiles are stored in armoured bunkers kilometres below the planet's surface.

IN45.554
Orb. Dist. 3.94AU
0.76G/Temp 2°C
Dead World
Tithe Grade: Adeptus Non
Aestimare: K500
Population: No indigenous
lifeforms recorded

BELIS C

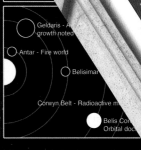

Geldaris -
growth noted

Antar - Fire world

Belisimar

Corwyn Belt - Radioactive m

Belis Cor
Orbital doc

AGRIPINAA

Virtually the entire surface of this world is covered with industrialised infrastructure, pipelines, factories, mines, refineries, processing plants and manufactorum cathedrals. Like almost every other inhabited planet in the sector, this world primarily produces materials for the Cadian front and its industrial heartland is solely engaged in the production of ammunition.

AM23.5
Orb. Dist. 2.4AU
0.77G/Temp 4°C
Industrial World
Tithe Grade:
Exactis Tertius
Aestimare: B30
Population: 80,000,000

AGRIPINAA SYSTEM

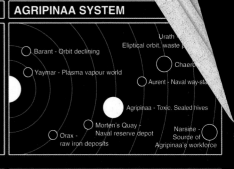

Urath -
Eliptical orbit. waste

Barant - Orbit declining

Yaymar - Plasma vapour world

Chaero

Aurent - Naval way-sta

Agripinaa - Toxic. Sealed hives

Orax -
raw iron deposits

Morten's Quay -
Naval reserve depot

Narsine -
Source of
Agripinaa's workforce

THRACIAN PRIMARIS

Planetary capital of Helican sub-sector, Thracian Primaris glows like an oozing cataracted eye. The planet has no moons and its populace live primarily in hive cities scattered across seven tenths of its surface. Defended by five Ramilies class starforts and with a PDF of 8 million men, the planet is as well defended as any Imperial world.

HSs 1.01
Orb. Dist. 0.89AU
1.12G/Temp 28°C
Industrial World
Tithe Grade: Exactis
Particular
Aestimare: A350
Population: 22,000,000,000

THRACIAN PRIMARIS SYSTEM

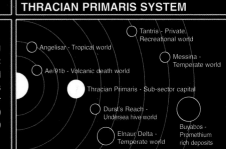

Tantris - Private
Recreational world

Angelisar - Tropical world

Messina -
Temperate world

Ae/91b - Volcanic death world

Thracian Primaris - Sub-sector capital

Durst's Reach -
Undersea hive world

Buyabos -
Promethium
rich deposits

Elnaur Delta -
Temperate world

CHINCHARE

(Rogue Systems) – An asteroid locked in a figure of eight orbit around a binary star. Once home to a creature of Chaos formed from the coagulated bodies of pilgrims who had descended into the asteroid to worship a corrupted crystal structure known as the Lith. The creature was destroyed by Inquisitor Eisenhorn and Magos Bure.

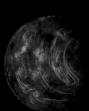

AM3.04
Orb. Dist. 2.44AU
0.5 – 9.67G/Temp 12°C
Mining World
Tithe Grade: Adeptus Non
Aestimare: G130
Population: Skeleton crew of
miners and associated staff.

CHINCHARE SYSTEM

Utolian - Ravaged by plasma storms

Van Seles's world - Abandoned

Plessern - Harvestable
plasma storms

Sabbatorus -
Sector producer
of plasma drives

Chinchare - Mining world (contact lost)

Orthrea -
Hollow world

XV/428 - Waste world of Sabbatorus

HYDRA CORDATUS

A collection of blighted worlds that have remained quarantined for many centuries following the discovery of xenos artefacts buried beneath their surfaces. It is suspected that these may be similar in nature to the monolithic black pylons as found on the surface of Cadia. Imperial Fist vessel *Justita Fides* listed as missing after its failure to arrive at Hydraphur following a warp jump from Hydra Cordatus.

OM01.876
Orb. Dist. 2.06 – 8.74AU
Mean Gravity 0.94G
Mean Temp 34°C
Dead World
Tithe Grade: Adeptus Non
Aestimare: Z1
Population:
Index Expurgatorius

HYDRA CORDATUS SYSTEM

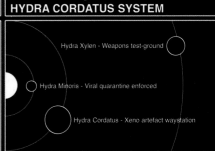

Hydra Xylen - Weapons test-ground

Hydra Minoris - Viral quarantine enforced

Hydra Cordatus - Xeno artefact waystation

CADIAN SHOCK TROOPS

reputation for martial prowess and courage, Cadian Shock Troops are a force to be feared.
ning all the battle formations that are typical of the Imperial Guard, Cadian armies favour the
on of the Kasrkin as well as the use of cadets from the Youth Army.

Lord Castellan Ursarkar E. Creed leads Cadia in its long war against the perils of the Eye of Terror.

Cadets in the Cadian army are trained in the arts of war from an early age and each yearns for the opportunity to test his bravery under fire. Youth Army squads, or 'Whiteshields', regularly see combat before they are fully trained.

Standing resolutely against the tide of Chaos, the Cadian Shock Troops prepare to hold the line.

The Commissar is a brooding, remote figure in the Imperial army. To denote his rank and position he wears a black dress uniform.

The elite Kasrkin are trained to the highest standards and are utterly loyal to Cadia.

Scouting ahead of the Cadian formations, the Sentinel has proved itself time and again as an indispensible mobile weapon of war.

ULTHWÉ STRIKE FORCE

Unable to ignore the threat of Chaos, Eldrad Ulthran summons the forces of the Ulthwé Craftworld to add their strength to the conflict. Grim and forbidding, the Eldar have donned their black armour and taken up their weapons to strike down all who stand before them.

The feared Seer Council has arrayed itself for battle and marched forth in the name of Ulthwé. Bearing deadly psychic weaponry, the Farseer and his bodyguard are opponents to be feared.

Armed with a Singing Spear, this converted Warlock of the Seer Council rides a jetbike into battle.

The implacable Necrons face the swift assault of the Ulthwé Strike Force.

This black armour mirrors the brooding and warlike character of the Guardians of Ulthwé. Armed with close combat weapons, the Storm Squads attack without mercy all who would threaten the Webway.

BLACK GUARDIANS

● The base colour of the armour is Chaos Black.

◐ This was highlighted with Codex Grey.

○ Bleached Bone was applied as a contrast colour on the weapons and helmets.

CONVERSIONS - MUTANTS

When it comes to making Mutants, the rules are, there are no rules! To begin with you can mix together parts from a couple of different sprues to make your creatures. We started with Imperial Guardsmen as the basis for the Mutants and began adding parts from different sprues.

Zombies sprue - Zombie parts are generally shrivelled and rotting, making them perfect for not only Mutants, but Plague Zombies too. These contrast well with large limbs, such as those of Orks.

Their clothing and weapons are very primitive and feral. Contrast these with a high-tech weapon or uniform.

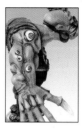

Mutation sprue - The wealth of arms and heads on the Chaos Mutation sprue means that even the simplest addition from the sprue can make all the difference.

Orks sprue - You can get massive muscular arms, legs and torsos from an Ork sprue. The Ork head itself is so huge it has been used as a torso on this Mutant.

Marauder sprue - An alternative to using an Imperial Guardsman as the basis for Mutant building is to use instead the medieval and barbaric Marauder of Chaos.

Big Muties - There are literally hundreds of metal monsters in the Citadel Miniatures range that you can make use of.

Mix and match parts from Rat Ogres, Daemon Princes and even Chaos Spawn. There is a whole catalogue of parts on offer and you can add plastic parts, including the Mutation sprue, to really finish off a model.

13TH COMPANY CONVERSIONS

Make 13th Company Space Marines by combining parts from Space Wolves sprues with Chaos Space Marines. Use any parts you wish, just avoid any Chaos iconography: the Chaos star and any Chapter badges. How many parts you use is up to you – 50/50 is about right.

CONVERTING CHAOS TRAITORS

One way to make a Traitor is to use the Imperial Guardsmen as the basis – they look better if they have a more piratical, barbaric look. Try adding parts from the Marauder of Chaos sprue, in particular the heads and animal skins.

This Leman Russ tank is part of a Traitor's arsenal. It has parts from the Chaos tank and vehicle accessory sprue added to the hull, as well as to the tank's weapons.

CHARACTERS FROM THE EYE OF TERROR CAMPAIGN

Ahriman of the Thousand Sons

Abaddon the Despoiler

Typhus

The Avatar of the Bloody-handed God

*Eldrad Ulthran,
Farseer of Ulthwé*

Maugan Ra

Logan Grimnar

*Lord Castellan
Ursarkar E. Creed*

*Commander Azrael, Supreme Grand
Master of the Dark Angels.*

FIGHTING THE EYE OF TERROR CAMPAIGN

This section of the book contains all you need to take part in one of the most apocalyptic battles ever to affect the Imperium. Whether the forces of Chaos conquer and destroy countless Imperial worlds or whether they are cast howling back into the hell of the Eye itself is a dilemma that can only be resolved by plenty of games of Warhammer 40,000!

On the pages that follow, you will find four new army lists to use in these games based on the forces immersed in the heat of battle during Abaddon's Thirteenth Black Crusade. You will also find ideas for battles that include these forces and many more, allowing you to create a storyline behind each of your games. Of course, the Eye of Terror is so vast that it blights a region of space many light-years across, and the sheer number of forces involved are too massive to catalogue accurately. Therefore you can use any of the published Codexes to fight in the campaign. Obvious contenders are the Imperial Guard, Space Marines, Space Wolves, Dark Angels, Blood Angels, Eldar, Dark Eldar and of course Daemonhunters and Chaos Space Marines. The Necron threat is not to be underestimated, although their motives are as alien as their arcane weaponry. The Tau and the Orks, although not directly involved, could both fight for the Imperium or Chaos respectively. As for the Tyranids, they really don't need any excuse for fighting, and the tendrils of the hive fleets are multiplying with every passing year.

Codex: Eye of Terror also offers a unique opportunity to use some of the special characters shown opposite in your battles, and perhaps build a storyline around their heroics or foul deeds. In particular, Abaddon and Typhus from Codex: Chaos Space Marines, Eldrad Ulthran and Maugan Ra from Codex: Eldar and Logan Grimnar from Codex: Space Wolves are all in the thick of the action, and, along with Ursarkar Creed, should make an appearance in more than the occasional game.

As the more hard-bitten gamers out there will realise, perhaps the most exciting opportunity provided by this book is to try out four brand new armies in your games of Warhammer 40,000. Why not try them against each other as well as against the army lists in previously published Codexes?

USING THE NEW ARMY LISTS

Not only can these army lists be used during the Eye of Terror campaign, but they can also be used for 'ordinary' games of Warhammer 40,000 as well. However, they are not complete lists in their own right, unlike many army lists published in previous Codexes. Each of these lists is used in conjunction with another army list, as shown on the table below. For example, if you wanted to field an Ulthwé Strike Force, you would use the new list presented here along with the army list in Codex: Eldar. Unless noted otherwise in this volume, all rules, options and limitations that apply to the army chosen from the original Codex also apply to the new army.

ARMY	CODEX REQUIRED
Cadian Shock Troops	Codex: Imperial Guard
The Lost and the Damned	Codex: Chaos Space Marines
Ulthwé Strike Force	Codex: Eldar
The 13th Company	Codex: Space Wolves and Codex: Space Marines

When you are choosing your army, you may make choices from the options presented in the following lists, within the normal limitations of the Force Organisation chart being used, points value of the battle, etc. Some of the entries that follow replace an entry or option from the original Codex, while some options from the Codex may not be allowed with the new army. If this is the case, you may only use the entry or option presented in this Codex.

The fate of the Imperium hangs in the balance. The forces of the Despoiler stand poised to deliver the deathblow to the Cadian sector and pour forth from the Eye of Terror to wage endless war on the Emperor's realm. Now you can take part in the battles that will decide whether the Cadian Gate will fall to Abaddon or whether its brave defenders are able to repulse his massive invasion.

The Eye of Terror campaign spans a multitude of sectors of the Imperium and there are battles of all sizes raging, from system-spanning conflicts involving hundreds of regiments and battle fleets, to the actions of individual squads of soldiers, or even lone Inquisitors. This diversity enables you to play any size of game you like, and also allows you to fight battles using the different game systems set in the Warhammer 40,000 universe. As well as playing Warhammer 40,000, you can devise games of Battlefleet Gothic, Inquisitor and Epic 40,000 to capture every aspect of Abaddon's Thirteenth Black Crusade.

Not only that, but the sheer diversity of worlds and sectors being fought over enables you to play games on any scenery imaginable. The sectors surrounding the Eye of Terror include an almost limitless potential of world types: hive worlds, ice worlds, desolate ruins or anything else your imagination can conjure, so it doesn't matter what scenery you have available, you'll be able to replicate the battlefields of the Eye of Terror. Remember, the army lists presented in this book are not the only forces fighting; there are huge numbers of other Imperial Guard regiments, Space Marine Chapters, Chaos warbands and cults involved in the campaign as well as Eldar and Necron forces. Many of the forces involved also employ the dubious services of mercenaries, so almost any army can be fielded.

In a warzone of this size, there are innumerable types of battle being fought, from nightmare sieges of Imperial fortifications, gruelling trench warfare, sweeping battles across desert plains or small-scale skirmishes on space stations between warring Space Marines. Hopefully, the background presented in this book will give you plenty of ideas for games, whether they are one-off battles or vast, linked campaigns. One-off games are fun, but it's always more involving to feel that your victories have an impact on a larger scale and campaigns are a great way of achieving this. For example, your gaming group could fight battles revolving around the siege of the hives of Subiaco Diablo by the hordes of Chaos and shambling Plague Zombies. Games could involve the fight to recapture a military base that has fallen into Chaos hands. Victory or defeat would have consequences for both sides and will lead to other battles being fought as the campaign progresses. Other games might involve the defence of a Medicae facility treating the victims of the Plague of Unbelief, which, if it falls, swells the ranks of the Chaos player in the next game. These are just a few examples of what you can do, and campaigns such as this add a great depth to your games when there is something at stake other than your own kudos.

White Dwarf and the Games Workshop website (www.eyeofterror.com) will be keeping you up to date with all the happenings throughout the warzones and, while the campaign runs, your gaming group's battles can play a part in deciding the fate of a particular world, or even sector.

The fate of the Imperium is in your hands.

SPACE WOLVES 13TH COMPANY

The legendary 13th Great Company of the Space Wolves Legion disappeared 10,000 years ago, and the circumstances of that disappearance are the subject of numerous myths and legends. With the advent of the Thirteenth Black Crusade, Abaddon has unleashed the hordes of the Eye of Terror upon Mankind. Snapping at his heels come elements of the 13th Company, warbands intent upon fulfilling the task they were set ten millennia past by, legend states, the Primarch Leman Russ himself.

A Space Wolves 13th Company warband uses the following units:

HQ	1 Wolf Lord*; 0-1 Rune Priest*; 0-1 Wolf Priest*.
ELITES	Wulfen pack; Storm Claws pack
TROOPS	Grey Slayers pack
FAST ATTACK	Fenrisian Wolf pack; Storm Claws Biker pack
HEAVY SUPPORT	13th Company Long Fangs pack

* These units are chosen from Codex: Space Wolves; the remainder are from the 13th Company list.

The Space Wolves' 'Retinues' special rule applies to the 13th Company. Those characters that can take bodyguards are noted in this list; Wolf Guard bodyguards are not available to them.

A 13th Company army is never joined by allies or units from other lists, for example, Deathwatch Space Marines, Inquisitors or Assassins. None of the 13th Company have access to, or may make use of, transports of any type.

SPECIAL RULES

A 13th Company warband makes use of the special rules as described in Codex: Space Marines and Codex: Space Wolves, except that they may not use the *Drop Pods* special rule. They also use the new rules below:

Move through cover: All members of the 13th Company, with the exception of packs of Fenrisian Wolves and Storm Claws biker packs roll an extra D6 when rolling to move through difficult terrain. In most circumstances this will mean that they roll 3D6 and pick the dice with the highest score. Models in Terminator armour, and any packs they lead, do not benefit from this ability.

Scouts: The Space Marines of the 13th Company are adept at catching an enemy unawares. To represent this, the entire army may always be deployed at the start of the battle, even in scenarios where you would normally be required to hold models in reserve. In addition, after both sides have deployed the army may make a 'free move'. This move happens before the first turn takes place, before deciding who has the first turn, and all normal movement rules apply. In this case, Wulfen do not move subject to the *Animal Rage* rule, and a Rune Priest may not use The Gate. Models in Terminator armour, and any packs they lead do not get the free move, and neither do Storm Claws biker packs (due to the noise they make!).

Sentries: In scenarios which use the *Sentries* scenario special rule, a 13th Company warband uses four Grey Slayers as sentries, each having a spotting range of twice its Initiative.

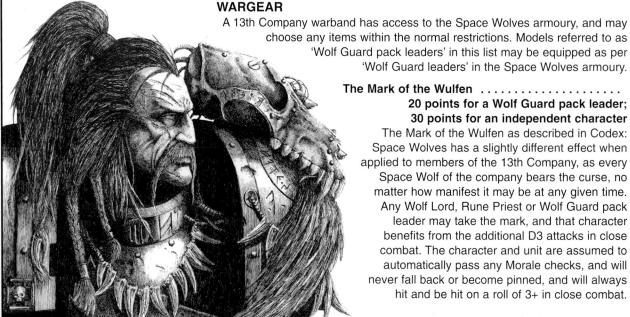

WARGEAR

A 13th Company warband has access to the Space Wolves armoury, and may choose any items within the normal restrictions. Models referred to as 'Wolf Guard pack leaders' in this list may be equipped as per 'Wolf Guard leaders' in the Space Wolves armoury.

The Mark of the Wulfen . . . .
20 points for a Wolf Guard pack leader;
30 points for an independent character
The Mark of the Wulfen as described in Codex: Space Wolves has a slightly different effect when applied to members of the 13th Company, as every Space Wolf of the company bears the curse, no matter how manifest it may be at any given time. Any Wolf Lord, Rune Priest or Wolf Guard pack leader may take the mark, and that character benefits from the additional D3 attacks in close combat. The character and unit are assumed to automatically pass any Morale checks, and will never fall back or become pinned, and will always hit and be hit on a roll of 3+ in close combat.

1 WOLF LORD

Bodyguard: The Wolf Lord may be accompanied by a bodyguard of Storm Claws, chosen from the Elites section of the army list. If chosen as a bodyguard, they count as part of the same HQ choice on the force organisation chart as the Wolf Lord. If the Wolf Lord is mounted on a bike, then he may instead take a bodyguard of Storm Claws bikers.

Wulfen Lord: If the Wolf Lord bears the Mark of the Wulfen, then Wulfen may be taken as Troops instead of Elites. In this case, Grey Slayers are not available to the army (as all but the hardiest of brethren have fallen to the curse of the Wulfen).

0-1 RUNE PRIEST

PSYCHIC POWER: The Gate

A Rune Priest of the 13th Company must guide his companions through the perils of the Eye of Terror. He has learned how to open small, temporary warp gates, through which he can pass in order to divine the path ahead.

On a successful Psychic test, the Rune Priest can use the power at the start of the Movement phase instead of moving normally. The Rune Priest and up to one squad of Grey Slayers, Storm Claws (not Storm Claws Bikers!) or Long Fangs within 6" of him is removed from the tabletop and then immediately placed anywhere on the tabletop using the Deep Strike rules. The Gate may be used even if enemy models are in base contact with the Rune Priest or any of the squad that move with him (the enemy models are left behind). This power replaces Stormcaller.

0-1 WOLF PRIEST

Wulfen-kind: If a Wolf Priest joins a Wulfen pack, you may choose whether or not it is subject to the *Animal Rage* rule each turn, so long as the Wolf Priest is with the pack. If the pack moves due to the *Animal Rage* rule, the Wolf Priest will move with them, but may not fire any weapons in the Shooting phase. A Wolf Priest may not take the Mark of the Wulfen.

HQ

Imperial observers believe the 13th Company has split into a number of smaller warbands, each forming the retinue of an individual Lord. Whether the warbands sighted to date represent a small proportion of the 13th Company's number is unknown, and it is entirely possible the bulk of the Company remains within the Eye of Terror. The leaders are mighty heroes who have led their bands throughout the many long centuries of their hunt, and some believe their quarry is now close at hand.

Exactly how the 13th Company navigate and travel through the Eye of Terror is a mystery, but some believe the Rune Priests hold the key. These warrior-mystics have been observed to traverse the battlefield by means of teleportation, and this psychic ability is thought by some to lie at the heart of the matter.

A Wolf Priest is often seen in the company of the Wulfen, those brothers of the 13th Company who have succumbed utterly to the curse of the Canis Helix. He is thought to act as a warden of the lost, the only one who can control them in battle, and temper their rage once victory is won.

WULFEN PACK

	Pts/Model	WS	BS	S	T	W	I	A	Ld	Sv
Wulfen	24	5	0	5	4	1	5	2+1	10	3+

Number/squad: 5-15

Weapons: Though some Wulfen may still bear the remnants of their former weaponry, they use only their savage claws in close combat, which are counted as two close combat weapons (included in the profile above).

SPECIAL RULES

Animal Rage: At the beginning of the 13th Company Movement phase, each Wulfen pack must advance a normal move +D6" towards the nearest enemy instead of moving normally. The extra D6" movement is not affected by difficult terrain.

Wolf Priest: No character other than a Wolf Priest may join a Wulfen Pack.

STORM CLAWS PACK

	Pts/Model	WS	BS	S	T	W	I	A	Ld	Sv
Storm Claws	21	4	4	4	4	1	4	2	9	3+
Wolf Guard	+10	4	4	4	4	1	4	3	9	3+

Number/squad: 6-10

Weapons: Bolt pistol and close combat weapon, frag and krak grenades.

Options: Up to two models may replace their close combat weapon with a power weapon at +10 points, or a power fist at +15 points. Up to two models may replace their bolt pistol with a plasma pistol at an additional cost of +10 points each.

Character: One Storm Claw may be upgraded to a Wolf Guard pack leader for +10 points. The leader may choose additional equipment from the Space Wolves armoury.

ELITES

Those brothers of the 13th Company upon whom the Curse of the Wulfen is fully manifest are banded together into packs of snarling, feral beasts. With matted pelts and voracious eyes, they stalk their prey as wild creatures, using only their animal claws to tear and rend them asunder.

Though all members of the 13th Company have reached the levels of skill in warcraft equivalent to a Space Wolves Wolf Guard, the Storm Claws are equipped to fully utilise these skills in hand-to-hand combat. They are savage and unrelenting, yet noble and stoic in pursuit of their mission.

TROOPS

At the core of the 13th Company are the Grey Slayers packs, men who have served for millennia and are as dependable and experienced on the field of battle as any mortal could aspire to be. These men have borne the Curse of the Wulfen for millennia, and through it survived the very worst the Eye of Terror can throw at them.

GREY SLAYERS PACK

	Pts/Model	WS	BS	S	T	W	I	A	Ld	Sv
Grey Slayers	21	4	4	4	4	1	4	2	9	3+
Wolf Guard	+10	4	4	4	4	1	4	3	9	3+

Number/squad: 6-10

Weapons: Bolter and close combat weapon, frag and krak grenades

Options: Up to two models may be equipped with one of the following weapons each: flamer at +6 points; melta gun at + 10 points; plasma gun at +10 points.

Character: One Grey Slayer may be upgraded to a Wolf Guard pack leader for +10 points. The leader may choose additional equipment from the Space Wolves armoury.

Standard Bearer: One Grey Slayer in the army may be upgraded to a Standard Bearer and given a wolf totem from the armoury at the cost listed there.

SPECIAL RULES
True Grit: The Grey Slayers have the strength and skill to fire a bolter with one hand and may use the 'True Grit' rule.

FAST ATTACK

The Space Wolves have always had an affinity with the creatures of the wild, and the brothers of the 13th Company of old were known to take them into battle with them. Today, the 13th Company are often accompanied by the descendents of these noble, savage beasts.

The 13th Company have been observed to use bikes to scout the battlefield and to probe enemy lines. They are used in battle to outmanoeuvre the enemy, harrying his flanks and disrupting his lines so that the Grey Slayers may advance uncontested. Caught between the two, the enemy is soon forced to attempt a desperate breakout lest he become completely cut off.

FENRISIAN WOLF PACK

	Pts/Model	WS	BS	S	T	W	I	A	Ld	Sv
Fenrisian Wolf	10	4	0	4	4	1	4	2	8	6+

Number/squad: 5-15

SPECIAL RULES
Cavalry: Fenrisian Wolves move as Cavalry. They must always charge and make a sweeping advance whenever possible.

STORM CLAWS BIKER PACK

	Pts/Model	WS	BS	S	T	W	I	A	Ld	Sv
Biker	36	4	4	4	4(5)	1	4	2	9	3+
Pack Leader	+10	4	4	4	4(5)	1	4	3	9	3+

Number/squad: 3-5 13th Company Space Wolves mounted on bikes.

Weapons: Each bike is fitted with twin-linked bolters. Each biker is armed with a close combat weapon, frag and krak grenades.

Options: Up to two models may be armed with one of the following: power weapon at +10 points; power fist at +15 points; flamer at +6 points; meltagun at +10 points; plasma gun at +10 points.

Character: One biker may be upgraded to a Wolf Guard pack leader for +10 points. The leader may choose additional equipment from the Space Wolves armoury.

SPECIAL RULES
Skilled Riders: Storm Claws bikers may re-roll a failed Difficult Terrain test, but must accept the result of the second roll.

HEAVY SUPPORT

Old and wise in the ways of war when the Imperium was young, the Long Fangs remain the voice of reason and sage council in a 13th Company warband as they do in the Space Wolves Chapter as a whole. They provide devastating fire support as their brethren advance, directing their volleys of las-blast and heavy bolter shell with unerring cunning.

13TH COMPANY LONG FANGS PACK

	Pts/Model	WS	BS	S	T	W	I	A	Ld	Sv
Long Fang	18	4	4	4	4	1	4	1	9	3+
Pack Leader	36	4	4	4	4	1	4	1	9	3+

Number/squad: Pack leader plus 2-4 Long Fangs

Weapons: The pack leader is armed with a bolt pistol and close combat weapon. Each remaining Long Fang must be armed with one of the following weapons each: heavy bolter at +15 points; missile launcher at +20 points; lascannon at + 35 points; plasma cannon at +35 points; flamer at +10 points; meltagun at +15 points; plasma gun at +15 points.

SPECIAL RULES
Fire Control: As long as the pack leader is alive and doesn't shoot in the Shooting phase or charge in the Assault phase then the pack may engage up to two different target units instead of one. Simply declare which models will fire at each target and then carry on using the normal rules.

CADIAN SHOCK TROOPS

The Imperial Guard contains countless regiments raised on innumerable worlds. Amongst these, several have achieved a glorious reputation in the Emperor's service. Few, if any have been as loyal, resourceful or courageous as the Cadian shock troops. Ever since the Horus Heresy, Cadia has guarded the entrance to the Eye of Terror and as a consequence the entire world is given over to mastering the art of battle and constructing weapons of war. In addition to guarding against Chaos, Cadian regiments have fought in thousands of Imperial Crusades and have served all over the Imperium. Even on the distant worlds of the Eastern Fringe there are colonies formed around the veterans of mustered-out Cadian regiments. Such is their reputation that many other regiments emulate their equipment and tactical doctrines, although few can match their prowess.

Cadian regiments campaigning away from Cadia for long periods will often fill their ranks with local recruits and may even include abhumans such as Ogryns in their formations. Such regiments use the standard Codex: Imperial Guard list. This list covers regiments that have maintained their links with their homeworld.

Cadian Shock Troops use the following units from Codex: Imperial Guard and from the new entries below:

HQ	1 Command Platoon* (with 0-2 Special Weapon Squads as part of the allowance of 0-5 support squads); 0-5 Commissars*; 0-5 Sanctioned Psykers
ELITES	Hardened Veteran Squads*; Kasrkin Squads (Use the Stormtrooper entry in Codex: Imperial Guard)
TROOPS	1+ Infantry Platoons*; Armoured Fist Squad*; 0-3 Kasrkin Squads (Use the Kasrkin entry below); Youth Army Platoons
FAST ATTACK	Sentinel Squadrons* (all variants including Cadian pattern below); Hellhounds*
HEAVY SUPPORT	Leman Russ*; Leman Russ Demolisher*; Basilisk*

* The profiles, rules and options for these units are found in Codex: Imperial Guard.

Cadians select their wargear and vehicle upgrades from Codex: Imperial Guard.

CADIAN SPECIAL RULES

IRON DISCIPLINE. Cadian nobles are raised from birth to be officers. They have an air of confidence and authority that keeps Cadian Regiments fighting to the last man. Any unit using the Leadership characteristic of a Cadian Officer (Colonel, Captain or Lieutenant) with the Iron Discipline ability for a Morale or Pinning test ignores the -1 modifier for being under half strength and may regroup even if below half strength. Cadian Officers may be given this ability for +5 points each.

SANCTIONED PSYKERS. Cadia is close to the Eye of Terror and has a high incidence of psychic activity. Some of these individuals exhibit enough control over their powers to provide support to the Shock Troops in battle. These sanctioned psykers will have one randomly determined power purchased from the list provided. Remember when selecting wargear that they are not officers.

KASRKIN. Cadia maintains several military academies based on the model set by the Schola Progenium. Exceptional individuals are trained at these establishments to Imperial Stormtrooper standards as Kasrkin (pronounced <u>Kas</u>-er-kin). Kasrkin squads are allocated to shock troop companies to provide an extra cutting edge in battle. See the army list summary and list entry for more details.

SHARPSHOOTERS. Cadians are formidable marksmen having undergone military training from an early age. Any Cadian infantry model with a BS of 3 may make a single re-roll of a shooting to hit roll of 1. No Cadian can miss that badly! The Sharpshooter ability has no effect when firing plasma weapons (which few men survive using long enough to master) or sniper rifles (where the slightest inaccuracy ruins the shot). This ability cost 10 points for a single squad (of any type).

> *"If it was a miracle then it was a Kantrael short-pattern nineteen-megathule Lasrifle miracle."*
> *General Karnow of the 122nd Cadian after his victory at Vogen*

YOUTH ARMY. Cadians are inducted into the military at an early age. Cadian armies may include Youth Army cadets. See the list entry below for more details.

SPECIAL WEAPON SQUADS. Cadian Shock Trooper Regiments may include squads of weapon specialists in their ranks. See the special weapon squad list entry for details. A Cadian army can include 0-2 special weapon squads as part of its command platoon but any used will count against the limit of five support squads.

CADIAN PATTERN SENTINEL

This is a regular Sentinel, armed with an autocannon instead of a multi-laser, and costing 45 points.

CADIAN WEAPONRY

Demolition Charges. Only one demolition charge can be used by a unit in any one turn. They have a range of 6". The attack is treated as an ordnance attack except that the model using the charge can move in the turn that it throws it. Place the ordnance blast marker normally and then roll to see if it scatters. Because of the short range this can be very hazardous to the user. Demolition charges are one-shot weapons. Once a model has used his demolition charge and survived, replace it with a model armed with a lasgun or a laspistol and close combat weapon. If such a substitute is not available remove the model instead.

	Range	Str	AP	Notes
Demolition Charge	6"	8	2	Ordnance

HQ

Sanctioned Psykers in Cadian regiments are haunted, gaunt individuals, tormented by nightmares of the Eye of Terror but strengthened by their faith in the Emperor and their duty to Cadia. Sanctioned Psykers provide vital defence against enemy mind tricks, an additional means of communication between units and occasionally a formidable and unexpected weapon.

A NOTE ON THE INTERNAL GUARD

The internal guard is Cadia's defence against Chaos cultist activity. It consists of Inquisitors of the Ordo Malleus permanently seconded to the Cadian military. Cadia's proximity to the Eye of Terror makes it particularly susceptible to corruption by the power of Chaos.

Like any other Imperial Guard army a Cadian army can select allied Daemonhunter units (see Codex: Daemonhunters for more details), in the case of the Cadians though these can be used to represent the Cadian Internal Guard. All Codex: Daemonhunter limitations apply. The Cadians get no special advantages when selecting allies from the Codex: Daemonhunter list, but it is mentioned here to inform players of a less well-known part of the Cadian military establishment that has considerable gaming potential. Naturally if an Inquisitor's retinue includes any veteran guardsmen it would be entirely appropriate to represent them with Kasrkin models.

'The place breeds recidivists like a pond breeds scum'

Inquisitor-General Neve on
Chaos cult activity on Cadia

0-5 SANCTIONED PSYKERS

	Pts/Model	WS	BS	S	T	W	I	A	Ld	Sv
Sanctioned Psyker	12	2	2	3	3	1	3	1	8	5+

Number/squad: You may include up to five Sanctioned Psykers in your army. These do not count as one of your HQ choices and may be taken in addition to your usual allocation of HQ units in a mission. Each Sanctioned Psyker must join a separate unit in the army as described below.

Weapons: Laspistol and close combat weapon.

Options: Sanctioned Psykers have access to the Imperial Guard armoury.

SPECIAL RULES

Psychic Powers. The Psyker will have one ability selected at random from those on the table below. Roll a D6 to determine which power the Psyker has.

It's for your own good. If a Sanctioned Psyker is attached to a unit which contains a Commissar and suffers a Perils of the Warp attack while using a psychic power, the Commissar will immediately execute him to prevent him being possessed. Remove the Psyker model as a casualty. The power he was attempting to use does not work.

Advisors. If used, one Sanctioned Psyker must be allocated to the Command HQ. Any others are allocated first to Platoon HQ Squads. If all Command and Platoon HQ's have a Sanctioned Psyker allocated to them the remainder are individually assigned to infantry platoon squads, armoured fist squads and Kasrkin squads.

SANCTIONED PSYKER POWERS

D6 Power Description

1 **No useable power.** The Psyker is disturbed by waking warp-spawned nightmares and does not dare to use his abilities at this time.

2 **Telepathic Order.** This power allows the sanctioned psyker to extend the zone of influence of an Officer he is accompanying. Use at the start of the Cadian turn. If the psychic test is passed the Leadership radius of an officer in the same squad as a sanctioned psyker using this power is extended to 18" until the start of the next Cadian turn.

3 **Psychic ward.** Sanctioned psykers are particularly useful in countering the heretical abilities of aliens and traitor scum. If a psychic power would normally affect the Sanctioned Psyker or the unit he is accompanying make a psychic test, if the test is passed, roll D6. On a 4+ the power is cancelled.

4 **Lightning arc.** Lightning leaps from the Psyker's hands surrounding his body before being hurled at his enemies with a gesture. This power is used in the Cadian shooting phase instead of firing a normal weapon and requires a successful psychic test.

    Range 24"   Str 3   AP 6   Heavy D6.

5 **Psychic lash.** The sanctioned psyker focuses his powers on nearby opponents, mentally ripping open arteries and puncturing organs. Make a psychic test at the start of the Cadian assault phase, if successful the power is in effect until the start of the next Cadian assault phase. Psychic Lash can be used in a close combat when the psyker would normally be able to make at least one attack. Instead of attacking normally the psyker gets D3 attacks (with no bonuses for charging, additional weapons etc) at S3 with any wounds ignoring armour saves (even if the target is not in base to base contact with the psyker).

6 **Machine curse.** The Sanctioned Psyker presses his hands against an enemy vehicle and calls upon his powers to pronounce a curse on the machine spirits of his enemies. This power is used in any Assault phase in place of normal attacks. Make the Psychic test at the start of the Cadian assault phase; if passed the power is effective until the end of the same Cadian assault phase. Make one attack against a vehicle in close combat, if a hit is scored roll D6. On a 1-3, the hit has no effect; on a 4-5, a glancing hit is caused, and on a 6, a penetrating hit is inflicted on the vehicle.

COMMAND PLATOON
0-2 CADIAN SPECIAL WEAPONS SQUAD..........35 PER SQUAD PLUS WEAPONS

	Pts/Model	WS	BS	S	T	W	I	A	Ld	Sv
Guardsmen	–	3	3	3	3	1	3	1	7	5+

Number/squad: 6 Guardsmen

Weapons: Lasgun or Laspistol and close combat weapon.

Options: The entire squad can be equipped with frag grenades at +6 points, krak grenades at +12 points or melta bombs at +24 points. Up to 3 Guardsmen can replace their weaponry with a weapon from the following list: meltagun at +15 points; flamer at +9 points; grenade launcher at +12 points; sniper rifle at +10 points; demolition charge at +10 points (maximum of one demolition charge per squad)

The Cadian Shock Troops are frequently called upon to assault formidable positions or to defend against overwhelming odds. To improve their chances they have learned to group men with specialist weapon skills in support units. These units perform tasks such as destroying bunkers, hunting tanks, blowing up bridges and so on.

TROOPS

KASRKIN SQUAD

	Pts/Model	WS	BS	S	T	W	I	A	Ld	Sv
Veteran Kasrkin Sergeant	16	3	4	3	3	1	3	2	8	4+
Kasrkin	10	3	4	3	3	1	3	1	8	4+

Number/squad: Each Kasrkin Squad consists of a Veteran Sergeant and four to nine Kasrkin.

Weapons: Hellgun, krak grenades and frag grenades. The Sergeant may replace his hellgun with hellpistol and close combat weapon.

Options: Up to 2 Kasrkin can replace their Hellguns with either a flamer at +6 points, a meltagun at + 10 points, a plasma gun at +10 points or a grenade launcher at +8 points. The squad may be given melta bombs at +4 points per model. One model may be upgraded to a Vox Operator with a comm-link (also known as a vox-caster) at +5 points.

Character: The Veteran Sergeant has access to the Imperial Guard armoury.

Transport: The squad may be mounted in a Chimera at +70 points. See the Chimera transport entry in Codex: Imperial Guard for more details.

The Kasrkin are the elite of the Cadian military, They are marked out while they are still in the Youth armies and enrolled in special academies where they receive training that is more than a match for that provided to Imperial Stormtroopers. They are utterly dedicated to the preservation of Cadia and follow an ethos of duty and honour that is both impressive and intimidating.

YOUTH ARMY PLATOON
2-5 SQUADS PER PLATOON ....40 POINTS PER SQUAD PLUS WEAPONS

A Youth Army Platoon consists of 2 to 5 squads of Cadets. The whole platoon functions as a single unit. This means that it will fight as a single unit (that's right – like one huge squad) of from 20 to 50 models. The squad organisation is only important in determining how many special and heavy weapons may be used.

Up to one Youth Army platoon may be used for each normal Infantry Platoon. This is the unit the Cadets will be recruited into when they have proven themselves. Youth Army Platoons are ignored when determining how many armoured fist squads can be fielded.

	Pts/Model	WS	BS	S	T	W	I	A	Ld	Sv
Cadet	–	2	2	3	3	1	3	1	5	5+

Squads: each squad in the platoon will be made up as follows:

Number/squad: 10 Youth Army Cadets.

Weapons: Youth army cadets have lasguns.

Options: Up to one youth army cadet per squad may be armed with a flamer at +9 points or a grenade launcher at +12 points. Up to two youth army cadets per squad may form a heavy weapons team with a heavy bolter at +15 points, a missile launcher at +20 points or an autocannon at +20 points.

The Cadian Youth Armies are teenage cadets. They spend much of their time training at a castellum in the wilderness, drilling under the supervision of Shock Troopers and fighting mock battles with other youth armies. This prepares them superbly for life in the Shock Troop regiments. There is no hesitation in testing the youth armies in the crucible of battle and every Cadet yearns to be recognised for his courage and recruited into the shock troops. Serving shock troops sometimes refer to the Youth Armies as 'whiteshields' because of the probationary Cadian badge they wear.

> "Any Cadian who can't field-strip his own lasgun by age ten was born on the wrong planet."
>
> Anon

LORD CASTELLAN URSARKAR E. CREED

The boy who was to become Lord Castellan Ursarkar E. Creed of Cadia was found in the war-racked ruins of Kasr Gallan by soldiers of the 8th Cadian Regiment. He would not speak of the horrors he had endured but his faith in the Emperor and his own will were already forged into a weapon of iron that he did not hesitate to use. Impressed by his courage and strength the 8th Regiment adopted him and he was inducted into the Youth Army or Whiteshield corps, and it was here he met Jarran Kell. The brooding Creed and garrulous Kell forged a bond that was to last for the rest of their lives. Already Creed was a natural leader and was driven by a fanatical devotion to the Imperial cause. Soon, his Whiteshield platoon was hurled into the five-year Drussite crusade, by the time the Cadian army celebrated victory in the blaze of the xeno-pyres Creed was a Captain of the Shock Troops and Kell his colour sergeant.

As an officer, Ursarkar Creed was demanding of his men and himself. His personal example earned him unconditional respect. In important matters he maintained the discipline expected of a Cadian unit but knew when to turn a blind eye, a quality that displeased many a Commissar. Creed rarely had to repeat an order; instead he exuded an intensity that compelled obedience from all around him. His greatest

strength though was his understanding of how a Cadian force should fight, not for him the unthinking exchange of lives so beloved of other Guard Officers. Creed mixed resolute defence with blistering counter-attacks, proving himself as capable of leading an army as a platoon.

With Kell ever at his side, Creed fought throughout the Hrud migration of 983-5.M41 and was commander of the force that hunted down the Chaos Space Marine Lord Brule on Trecondal. His first action as a Lord General of Cadia saw him not only defeat, but annihilate the Ulthwé raid on Aurent in 992.M41. By now he was Cadia's most successful living commander, and only his lowly birth held his career in check.

In 999.M41 a murderous plot by the forces of the great enemy killed several members of the Cadian High Command. In times of such dire emergency there existed a special military rank, Lord Castellan of Cadia, bestowed for life or until the emergency was over. Returning to Cadia from his latest campaign, Creed was met with massive acclaim from the rank and file of the Cadian army. One by one his potential rivals stepped down in the interests of unity until the foundling boy was, by common consent, appointed Lord Castellan of Cadia. In the dark days that followed he would need all his faith and all his skill.

Any Cadian army of at least 1,500 points may be led by Creed. Creed has always insisted that no officer should fear front-line duty and habitually lives up to his own words. His lifelong comrade Sergeant Jarran Kell always accompanies him to battle and is responsible for ensuring his survival. If the army Command Platoon has a Chimera Transport then Creed and Kell may commandeer it for their own use (the original owners have to walk). If so this must be declared before deployment commences.

Ursarkar Creed and Jarran Kell are always used together although on the battlefield, both are independent characters and can separate and join different units as desired. Both must be used as listed, occupying a single HQ slot on the Force Organisation Chart. The points cost listed is for both characters. Victory points are awarded on the basis of wounds inflicted on Creed only. No Victory points are scored for killing or wounding Kell.

URSARKAR CREED

	Points	WS	BS	S	T	W	I	A	Ld	Sv
Creed	125	4	4	3	3	3	4	3	10	4+

Wargear: Trademark Item (pistols), refractor field, carapace armour, two matched hellpistols (fire as twin-linked hellpistol, count as additional close combat weapon in close combat).

SPECIAL RULES
Iron Discipline.

Master Strategist. Where there is a choice of mission based on strategy rating, an army containing Creed may always choose the mission. Similarly they may either choose to win the dice roll for choice of table edge or request that the dice for the first turn are re-rolled.

COLOUR SERGEANT JARRAN KELL

	Points	WS	BS	S	T	W	I	A	Ld	Sv
Kell	-	5	5	3	3	3	4	3	8	4+

Where Creed is silent and calculating, Kell is his voice, roaring and bombastic as only a colour sergeant can be. He has made keeping Creed alive his life's work and has the wounds to prove it. A fearsome fighter, his amplified voice drowns out the warcries of the enemy and ensures that Creed's orders are obeyed in the heat of battle. Although nominally a sergeant, Kell has all the privileges of being an officer including the Command special rule.

Wargear: Medallion Crimson, carapace armour, regimental banner, power fist, power sword. The regimental banner is that of the 8th Cadian regiment, and counts as the one regimental banner allowed in the army.

SPECIAL RULES
Iron Discipline.

Medallion Crimson. The Medallion Crimson is awarded to men who have suffered the most horrific injuries and have not lost their faith in the Emperor or their will to fight on. It takes a lot to stop a man who has earned this decoration. The first time the bearer is wounded by an attack that causes instant death he just takes a single wound instead.

Bodyguard. If within 2" of Creed, then Kell may change places with him at the start of either player's Assault phase. He will then fight Creed's opponents and Creed will fight his (if any).

> What do I ask of my officers? Merely that they do their duty with fire in their bellies and a prayer on their lips.
>
> Lord Castellan Ursarkar E. Creed

URSARKAR CREED DIRECTS THE DESTRUCTION OF THE VOLSCANI CATAPHRACTS AT THE BATTLE OF TYROK FIELDS

THE LOST AND THE DAMNED

The insane gods of Chaos have many, many servants; daemons large and small, mortal slaves which inhabit the Daemon worlds and give endless praise to their dark masters through toil, bloodshed and sacrifice and the Chaos Space Marines, ever wilful and ever the most favoured of all. An army of the Lost and the Damned represents a combined force of Chaos featuring all of these elements. Such forces will be commanded by powerful Chaos Space Marines, Daemon princes or some other great Demagogue, Traitor or Arch Heretic who's caught the eye of the Chaos powers. Their armies are often insane personal creations pursuing a path of strategy and tactics which defies rational military explanation. Their followers may be disciplined and well armed, backed with prodigious amounts of armour and firepower or a teeming horde of primitively armed mutants, monsters and daemons. The seemingly insane, unpredictable assaults of such Chaos forces are a nightmare for strategic planners and lowly troopers alike.

THE CHAOS HORDE ARMY LIST

The Chaos Horde army list uses the following units from Codex: Chaos Space Marines, Codex: Imperial Guard and the new entries below. Note: Codex: Imperial Guard is only needed if you wish to include Traitor Fast Attack and Heavy Support units. This list will work perfectly well just using it as an adjunct to Codex: Chaos Space Marines.

HQ	Arch Heretic (counts as Chaos Lieutenant/Sorcerer); Chaos Space Marine Aspiring Champions; Greater Daemon.
ELITES	Big Mutants; Possessed; Daemon packs.
TROOPS	Traitors; Mutants (including Plague Zombies); Gibbering Hordes (counts as Nurglings)
FAST ATTACK	Chaos hounds; Daemonic Beasts; Traitor Recon (Sentinels, Roughriders, Hellhound)*
HEAVY SUPPORT	Defiler; Chaos Spawn; Traitor tank (Leman Russ Battle Tank, Basilisk)*

A maximum one Traitor Recon or Tank unit may be chosen per Troops choice of Traitors in the army.

Notes: Units of Traitor troops taken as compulsory choices on the force organisation chart must be maximum strength. Units of Gibbering hordes are not restricted to the number of units with the Mark of Nurgle in the army as they represent lesser spawn, minor daemons and a host of other hell-spawned nastiness.

The Lost and The Damned may include the following allied units from Codex: Chaos Space Marines. 0-1 HQ choice, 0-1 Elite choice, 0-2 Troops choices, 0-1 Fast Attack choice. Allied units may not be used as compulsory choices on the force organisation chart. Units with a Mark of Chaos are always Elites choices.

SPECIAL RULES

Strategy Rating: The Lost and the Damned have a strategy rating equal to the roll of a D3.

Sentries: A Lost and the Damned Army uses 10 Traitors or Mutants as sentries in scenarios that require them.

Icons and Daemon summoning: The Lost and The Damned often call forth Daemons onto the battlefield. All the rules in Codex: Chaos Space Marines apply to Daemon summoning by the Lost and The Damned. Traitor and mutant units can be upgraded to include Chaos icons to enable Daemon summoning. Agitators and Bosses may not be Daemonvessels.

Veteran Skills: Only Chaos Space Marine units can choose veteran skills.

Legion Rules: Specific Chaos Legion rules only apply to Chaos Space Marine units and characters of that Legion, not any other Lost and Damned units.

Vehicle upgrades: Vehicles in a Lost and Damned force can only use vehicle upgrades from their 'parent' Codex. For example, a Chaos Defiler can only use upgrades from Codex: Chaos Space Marines while Traitor Leman Russ can only choose upgrades from Codex: Imperial Guard.

NEW WEAPONS

Firearms: The dizzying profusion of fiendish weapons used by the minions of Chaos defy strict definition, be they warp-fueled arquebus or semi-organic machine pistols. As such they are categorized as 'Firearms' with the following characteristics.

	Range	Str	AP	Notes
Firearms	24"	4	6	Rapid fire; gets hot!*

*As plasma weapons.

Heavy stubber: Popular among the kind of low grade scum that make up the traitor hordes of Chaos legions, heavy stubbers are often stolen from planetary defence force armouries or crudely fabricated among the Daemon worlds of the Eye.

	Range	Str	AP	Notes
Heavy Stubber	36"	4	6	Heavy 3 (Assault 3 when used by Big Mutants)

CHAOS SPACE MARINE ASPIRING CHAMPION

	Pts/Model	WS	BS	S	T	W	I	A	Ld	Sv
Champion	27	4	4	4	4	1	4	2	10	3+

Number/squad: 1-3. You may include between 1 and 3 Champions as a single HQ choice. Each Champion must be allocated to lead a unit of Traitors or Mutants prior to deployment.

Weapons: Bolt pistol and close combat weapon or bolter.

Character: Each Champion may be equipped with up to 75 points of items from the Chaos Space Marine armoury at the points cost indicated, with the exception of Marks of Chaos. Thanks to the Champion's rather more 'solo' career Marks of Chaos are altered as follows;

- Mark of Khorne (10 points): The Champion has 3 Attacks on his profile
- Mark of Nurgle (10 points): The Champion's Toughness is 5. The original value of 4 is used for calculating Instant Death.
- Mark of Slaanesh (5 points): The model's Initiative becomes 5.
- Mark of Tzeentch (10 points): Th Champion gains the Sorcerer ability.
- Mark of Chaos Undivided (20 points): Re-roll Morale checks.

Note: With the exception of the Mark of Chaos Undivided, the Mark of Chaos is not applied to the unit the Champion is leading. A Champion with a Mark of Chaos may access Gifts of the Gods from their patron god.

HQ

Not all Chaos Space Marines choose to remain with their Legion eternally. Personal ambition, vendettas, jealousies, rivalries or the commands of their patrons may set their feet on a very different path. It is easy enough for such powerful warriors to quickly rise to the role of war chief, tyrant or despot to the lesser minions of Chaos.

BIG MUTANTS

	Pts/Model	WS	BS	S	T	W	I	A	Ld	Sv
Big Mutant	25	4	2	6	4	3	3	2	7	5+
Boss Mutant	+30	4	2	6	4	4	4	3	8	5+

Number/squad: 3-10

Weapons: Teeth, claws, bodyweight. Some large blunt and/or sharp implements.

Options: The squad can be equipped with firearms for +2 points per model. Up to two models in the squad may be upgraded to count as carrying a flamer at +6 points per model or a heavy stubber at +5 points per model. The squad can be upgraded to be scaly (4+ saving throw -1 Initiative) for +5 points per model.

Character: For an additional cost of +30 points one of the mutants can be upgraded to a boss. This only gives him a better profile; he doesn't get to choose anything from the armoury (he can still take squad options).

ELITES

Mutation is rife among the legions of Chaos as the uncaring gods bestow their twisted blessings on their worshippers without rhyme or reason. Big mutants are the grossest examples of their kind, huge and thickly muscled with an intellect to match. Whether these creatures were originally human is almost impossible to tell now, some sport bestial heads, dragging knuckles and scaly hides which would be more at home on a Grox. In battle such creatures instinctively group together or may rally around a particularly loud and obnoxious mutant leader.

TROOPS

Traitors are those have turned from the Emperor's light and joined their fortunes with the servants of darkness. Mercenaries, pirates, deserters and renegades flock to the banners of a black crusade in the hopes of being rewarded for their perfidy with wealth, power and prestige. With the star of Chaos in the ascendent whole regiments, even entire worlds will turn traitor to survive and wring out their miserable lives a little longer. Some units are led by Chaos Space Marines attempting to build up their own legions, serving beneath a greater liege lord only as long as it serves their purposes. Traitors are typically well armed with weaponry stolen and scavenged from a variety of sources, and have not yet descended so far into madness that their skills are completely lost.

The vast bulk of most Chaos legions is made up of a scrofulous tide of hideous mutants. These are the dregs of the Daemon Worlds within the Eye of Terror where uncounted billions raise their harsh voices in insane prayers to unspeakable horrors. The fiercest and least crippled of these fight for a place aboard the Chaos fleets as they go to war, hoping only to slay and plunder in their masters name and perhaps earn the favour of the fickle gods of Chaos. On occasion such dregs may be led by a Chaos Space Marine: blessed as they are with the twisting gifts of the gods, such a mighty warrior is worshipped as a messiah.

Plague Zombies

To represent the hordes of Plague Zombies unleashed during the Thirteenth Crusade, use Mutants with the Bloated Blessing of Nurgle. Zombies may not take any weapon upgrades or include a Boss. They are however, Fearless, and hence will automatically pass any Morale or Leadership test and cannot be Pinned. Because of their shambling gait, they will always move as if they are in difficult terrain.

TRAITORS

	Pts/Model	WS	BS	S	T	W	I	A	Ld	Sv
Traitor	8	3	3	3	3	1	3	1	6	5+
Agitator	+10	3	3	3	3	1	3	2	7	5+

Number/squad: 5-15

Weapons: Lasgun and frag grenades.

Options: Any model may exchange their lasgun for an autogun, shotgun or laspistol/autopistol and close combat weapon for free. Up to one model may be upgraded to an icon bearer for +5 points. Up to one model may exchange their weapon for a flamer at +3 points, a meltagun at +10 points, a sniper rifle at +5 points, a plasma gun at +10 points, a heavy stubber at +10 points or a grenade launcher at +10 points. Two traitors can form a weapon team with one of the following; a heavy bolter at +10 points, a lascannon at +20 points, an autocannon at +15 points, mortar at +15 points or a missile launcher at +15 points. The squad can be equipped with krak grenades for +2 points per model.

Character: For an additional cost of +10 points one Traitor may be upgraded to an Agitator. The character may purchase up to 15 points worth of weapons and wargear allowed by the Codex: Chaos Space Marine armoury (but no Marks, Gifts or other items).

Transport vehicle: Traitor squads numbering 10 models or less and not led by a Champion in Terminator armour may be mounted in a Rhino (counting as having BS 3) at an additional cost of +50 points or a Chimera at +70 points. Units mounted in this way become Fast Attack instead of Troops choices.

SPECIAL RULES.

Infiltrate: Traitors are often familiar with local conditions and defences, and are adept at using treachery to win tactical advantages. To represent this Traitors not led by a Chaos Space Marine Champion counts as having the Infiltrators veteran skill as described in Codex: Chaos Space Marines p19.

MUTANTS

	Pts/Model	WS	BS	S	T	W	I	A	Ld	Sv
Mutant	6	3	2	3	3(4)	1	3	1(2)	7	5+
Mutant Boss	+10	3	2	3	3(4)	2	3	2(3)	8	5+

Number/squad: 15-30

Weapons: A variety of crude blades, spears, basic pistols, bombs, clubs and pointed sticks which count as one (yes just one) Close combat weapon and frag grenades.

Options: The squad can replace their close combat weapons with firearms for free or replace their close combat weapons with an autopistol or laspistol for +1 points per model. The squad can be equipped with krak grenades for +2 points per model. Up to three models may be upgraded to an icon bearer for +3 points each. Up to two models in the squad may be upgraded to being armed with a flamer equivalent at +3 points per model or a heavy stubber at +5 points per model.

Character: For an additional cost of +10 points one of the Mutants may be upgraded to a Mutant Boss. The boss may purchase up to 15 points worth of weapons and wargear allowed by the Chaos Space Marine armoury (but no Marks, Gifts or other items).

Blessings of the gods: These count as the equivalent of Daemonic gifts as detailed in Codex: Chaos Space Marines. Mutants already have Daemonic Resilience (+1 T) and (unsurprisingly) Daemonic Mutations (+1 A) included in their profiles above.

One of the following blessings is also available at the points cost shown per model, if any blessings are chosen they must be applied to the entire squad. Some blessings are particularly associated with certain powers, but they are not restricted to them alone and should not be confused with Marks of Chaos. No blessing may be taken more than once:

- **Bloated** (Nurglesque): +3 points per model, Armour save increased to 4+ .
- **Burly, brawny and/or goatheaded** (Khornate/Chaos Undivided): +3 points per model, counts as Daemonic Strength (+1 Strength)
- **Horrifying, hypnotic or brightly coloured** (Slaaneshi): +2 points per model. counts as Daemonic Visage (-1 Ld to enemy in assaults) .
- **Leaping, floating or winged** (Tzeentchian): +6 points per model, counts as Daemonic Speed (move as cavalry) .

CHAOS HOUNDS

	Pts/Model	WS	BS	S	T	W	I	A	Ld	Sv
Chaos Hound	10	4	0	4	4	1	4	2	8	6+

Number/squad: 5-10

Weapons: Teeth

SPECIAL RULES.

Cavalry: Chaos Hounds count as cavalry, see the Warhammer 40,000 rules for details.

FAST ATTACK

Chaos hounds embody the worst elements of a nightmare hunter. Their bodies are twisted and deformed by the power of the warp so that glistening flesh and muscle are visible through the rips and tears in their lumpen hides and matted hair. Despite their hideous appearance they are lithe and strong, their loping strides capable of catching a fleeing man in a few bounds, pulling them down to their inevitable doom in their shark-like maws.

CHAOS SPAWN

	Pts/Model	WS	BS	S	T	W	I	A	Ld	Sv
Chaos Spawn	20	3	0	5	5	2	3	D6	9	3+

Number/squad: 3-5

Weapons: Teeth, claws, tentacles, stingers, pseudopodia etc etc.

SPECIAL RULES.

Random attacks: Chaos spawn flail wildly with their twisted appendages in combat. To represent this they have a random number of attacks, determined by rolling a D6 per spawn at the start of each Assault phase when they are fighting.

Fearless: Chaos Spawn have long since lost any semblance of rational thoughts or sanity. As such they automatically pass any morale checks or pinning tests they are required to make.

Insanely stupid. Make a Leadership test for each spawn unit at the start of the Chaos player's turn. If the test is failed the Spawn do not move that turn and may not assault. Spawn which are already in an assault don't have to test to fight – they're not that stupid. Independent characters may not join units of Chaos Spawn.

HEAVY SUPPORT

To gain the attention of the Chaos gods is a supremely risky venture. It may lead to power and riches beyond measure, but it may equally result in the supplicant being reduced to something far less than a man by the corrupting gifts of Chaos. Chaos spawn are heaving, ever-changing masses of flesh, bone and gristle which really have no sane right to be moving around under their own power. But they do move and chase and eat and… well it all gets pretty ugly pretty quickly. Chaos legions use spawn as terror weapons, unleashing packs of them to hurl themselves at the enemy in a nightmare wave of hopping, drooling, tentacular madness.

ULTHWÉ STRIKE FORCE

At the end of the 41st millennium the runic readings of the Farseers were brimming with dire portents. Eldrad Ulthran's worst suspicions were confirmed when Maugan Ra strode through the Craftworld's main webway portal, accompanied by a massive bodyguard of Dark Reapers. The presence of the Phoenix Lord on Ulthwé affirmed the fact that the Craftworld was in great peril. Before the hour was out, the Seer Council and Maugan Ra began a council of war.

Behind the closed doors of the Spirit Chambers, the Farseers vainly probed the skeins of probability for a safe path through the coming storm. The sheer scale of the coming conflict was terrifying; the forces of the Mon-keigh and the minions of Chaos outnumbered the Eldar by millions to one. There was only one way Eldrad could feasibly alter the course of fate in so many theatres of such an apocalyptic war.

Whilst the Avatar of Ulthwé was awoken and the Spear of Khaine assembled to march with him to war, Eldrad fragmented his consciousness, storing a piece of his psyche in hundreds of sacred Waystones. Maugan Ra assembled the Black Guardians of Ulthwé, dividing them into small Strike Forces capable of travelling the convoluted labyrinth of the webway. With the leader of each detachment carrying a sacred Waystone, Eldrad could disperse his consciousness across the entire sector, guiding each Strike Force through the webway to the heart of each battle at exactly the right time and location. Maugan Ra's Dark Reaper bodyguard added to the strength of the Black Guardians in each Strike Force, and every member of the Craftworld who could don the mask of the Warlock did so to better lead their brethren.

When the storm broke, Ulthwé was ready to strike like the lightning.

ULTHWÉ STRIKE FORCE SPECIAL RULES

Webway Strike: At least half the units (rounding up) in any Ulthwé Strike Force must be kept in reserve and enter play through a Wraithgate as described below, regardless of mission. These units must be noted down before deployment. Regardless of the mission being played, any unit that carries a Wraithgate automatically begins on table following the usual deployment rules.

Ulthwé Strike Force troops that are falling back must do so towards the nearest Wraithgate if one has been placed. If they are unable to do so they will fall back as specified in the mission. If a model from a unit that is falling back passes through the Wraithgate the entire unit is removed from play as if they have left the table. If the only model left on the table carrying a Wraithgate is destroyed, the Wraithgate is placed with the central hole over the spot where the model died.

Tactical Withdrawal: The highly disciplined Black Guardian squads that comprise an Ulthwé Strike Force know full well that a tactical retreat to preserve their strength is often their only option, and will make fighting withdrawals to the webway rather than endanger their craftworld by dying where they stand. Black Guardians (including jetbikes and support weapons) that fall back due to casualties inflicted will not rally and must continue to fall back even if above half strength. Any squad that is removed from play in this way whilst still above half strength only counts for half the unit's victory points.

Light Infantry: The Ulthwé Strike Force cannot include any vehicles other than Vypers and War Walkers, as all other Eldar vehicles are too large to manoeuvre through the delicate capillaries of the webway without causing catastrophic damage.

Guardians of Ulthwé: Due to the comparative rarity of Aspect Warriors in the Ulthwé Craftworld, only one squad of Aspect Warriors can be included in each force. Dark Reapers do not count toward this limit. Note that the special character Maugan Ra may be taken without your opponent's consent (see the Phoenix Lords rules in Codex: Eldar).

ARMOURY

In addition to the armoury in Codex: Eldar, Ulthwé Strike Force Farseers and Warlocks can purchase the following items.

Wraithgate (50 Points)
This is a mobile form of the portal used by the Eldar to link together places via the webway. It may be activated by an unengaged model carrying it in the Shooting phase, instead of shooting or using Fleet of Foot that turn. Place a spare Blast marker in base contact with the model when it activates the Wraithgate. From then on Strike Force units entering play as reserves enter play from the Wraithgate template instead of entering on the table edge. There is no risk of scattering or being killed when travelling in this way, and the Wraithgate cannot be destroyed. Once activated, the Wraithgate remains in place and the model that was carrying it is free to move away. If a unit becomes available to enter play, but no Wraithgate has been opened, it automatically enters play the turn after the Wraithgate has been opened. Characters on jetbikes may not carry a Wraithgate. Wraithgates cannot be moved over and do not block line of sight.

Waystones (25 points, one per army)
A waystone is essentially a large spirit stone to which a portion of an Eldar's psyche can be imparted. By using these stones Eldrad Ulthran is able to guide each Strike Force through the webway, using the mind of a fellow psyker as a beacon, and coordinate their attacks. If a psyker still held in reserve has a waystone, one Reserve roll may be re-rolled per turn, whatever the result. Furthermore, by psychically attuning himself to the waystone, a psyker can channel the immense psychic power stored within it onto the battlefield. Once per game, the bearer may cast Eldritch Storm in addition to any other psychic powers he may have. This is cast automatically and may not be Augmented.

Psychic Power: Augment (5 points)
Ulthwé Warlocks may be given the Augment psychic power instead of one of the psychic powers listed in Codex: Eldar. It is used when a Farseer in the Seer Council successfully uses a psychic power. Unlike other Warlock powers, the Warlock must pass a Psychic test to use Augment. If the test is successful, the range of the Farseer's power is doubled. Remember that a Warlock can only use Augment once per turn and that each Farseer power can only be augmented once per turn, you cannot double the range and then further double it with a second Warlock. Note that the Warlock must remain in the Seer Council to use Augment. If any Warlock fails to augment a power, a second Warlock may attempt to augment the same power.

ULTHWÉ STRIKE FORCE ARMY LIST

You will only need a copy of Codex: Eldar to use this list.

HQ	0-1 Spear of Khaine; 0-1 Seer Council
ELITES	Dire Avengers*, Howling Banshees*, Fire Dragons*, Striking Scorpions*, Rangers
TROOPS	Black Guardian Storm Squad, Black Guardian Defender Squad
FAST ATTACK	Black Guardian Jetbike Squadron, Black Guardian Vyper Squadron, Swooping Hawks*
HEAVY SUPPORT	Black Guardian War Walker Squadron, Black Guardian Support Weapon Battery, Dark Reapers.

Remember, only one Aspect Warrior squad may be used per army, with the exception of Dark Reapers.

0-1 SPEAR OF KHAINE

	Pts/Model	WS	BS	S	T	W	I	A	Ld	Sv
Avatar	80	10	0	6	6	4	5	3	10	5+
Warlock	11	4	4	3	3	1	4	1	8	4+

Squad: The Spear of Khaine consists of an Avatar and a Warlock escort, and counts as a single HQ choice. The Avatar must be accompanied by from 2 to 5 Warlocks (see Codex: Eldar). You may detach Warlocks from the Spear of Khaine and attach them to Guardian squads, as detailed in the Codex: Eldar army list. However, you must leave at least two Warlocks in the Spear of Khaine.

Options: The Warlocks may be given any equipment allowed by the Craftworld Eldar Armoury. They must each be equipped with either a Singing Spear or a Witchblade.

Warlock Powers: Each Warlock must be given a single Warlock power at the points cost listed in the Eldar armoury.

Rune Armour: See the Wargear section for details.

SPECIAL RULES
Fearless: While the Avatar is on the table, the Spear of Khaine automatically passes any Morale or Pinning tests it has to make.

Avatar: All the special rules in the Avatar entry in Codex: Eldar apply to the Avatar in the Spear of Khaine, but he no longer counts as an independent character.

Designer's Note: Remember, statistics cannot be raised above 10 for any reason (the Avatar's Weapon Skill being affected by Enhance, for instance).

HQ

In the direst of circumstances, Ulthwé accompanies its Avatar with a bodyguard of senior battle-seers known as the Spear of Khaine. An integral part of the psychic choir that summons the Avatar to war, the Spear consists of Warlocks that have previously spent centuries on the path of the Warrior and have a strong psychic connection to the Avatar. In conjunction with the living incarnation of their god, the Spear of Khaine is a nigh unstoppable force on the battlefield.

0-1 SEER COUNCIL

	Pts/Model	WS	BS	S	T	W	I	A	Ld	Sv
Farseer	+40	5	5	3	4	3	5	1	10	4+
Warlock	+11	4	4	3	3	1	4	1	8	4+

Squad: The Seer Council forms a single unit consisting of 2 Farseers and 3 Warlocks at a cost of 90 points.

Options: Up to three extra Farseers can be added to the Seer Council for +40 points each. If Eldrad Ulthran is included in the army, he counts as a HQ choice as normal, but must join the Seer Council and remain with it throughout the game.

Any number of additional Warlocks may be added to the unit at +11 points per Warlock.

Any Farseer or Warlock may be given any equipment allowed from the Eldar Armoury except that Farseers may not be mounted on jetbikes (they are far too old and proud to go racing around the skies!).

SPECIAL RULES
Psychic Powers: Each Farseer must be given between one and four Farseer psychic powers for the points cost listed in the Eldar Armoury. Warlocks must be given one Warlock power from the Eldar Armoury.

Rune Armour: See the Wargear section of Codex: Eldar for details.

Detaching Warlocks: You may detach Warlocks from the Seer Council and attach them to Guardian squads, as detailed in the Codex: Eldar army list. However, you must leave at least three Warlocks in the Seer Council.

The strength of Ulthwé is ultimately its Seer Council. During times of major conflict, the Seer Council take a far more active role on the battlefield, divining the most influential warzone in which to add the might of their Craftworld and opening Wraithgates to allow their brethren to effect one of the lightning raids which characterise Ulthwé's military actions.

TROOPS

As they are a standing army rather than a militia, the Black Guardians have extra training in their chosen battle-skills, and are known throughout the regions around the Eye of Terror both as saviours and dreaded foes. An Ulthwé Strike force typically has several large units of Black Guardians, all of whom have been trained to maximise the use of the webway strike.

BLACK GUARDIAN DEFENDER SQUAD

Use the Guardian Defender Squad entry. However, Black Guardian Defenders have BS 4 and are subject to Tactical Withdrawal. The unit may be joined by a Warlock from the Seer Council or Spear of Khaine. They may not use a Wave Serpent transport.

BLACK GUARDIAN STORM SQUADS

Use the Guardian Storm Squad entry. However, Black Guardian Storm Squad members have WS 4 and are subject to Tactical Withdrawal. The unit may be joined by a Warlock from the Seer Council or Spear of Khaine. They may not use a Wave Serpent transport.

FAST ATTACK

The elite squadrons of Black Guardian Jetbikes are often the first to emerge from an open Wraithgate, bursting from the ether in a storm of electricity to harry the enemy lines with accurate shuriken catapult fire.

BLACK GUARDIAN JETBIKE SQUADRON

Use the Guardian Jetbike Squadron entry. However, Black Guardian Jetbikes have BS4 and are subject to Tactical Withdrawal. The unit may be joined by a Warlock from the Seer Council or Spear of Khaine.

0-1 SWOOPING HAWKS

Swooping Hawks that are kept in reserve may deploy either from the Wraithgate, in which case they may not use their Grenade Packs, or as detailed in the Swooping Hawk Wings entry in the Eldar armoury.

A Strike Force often uses its Vypers to take a position on the flank and rear of enemy tanks, picking the weakest spot in the enemy armour and crippling them with surgical strikes.

BLACK GUARDIAN VYPER SQUADRON

Use the Vyper Squadron entry. However, Black Guardian Vypers cost 60 points each and have BS4.

HEAVY SUPPORT

Strike Forces typically use their support weapons to pin enemy forces in place until the webway strike is launched. The formidable arsenal carried by the highly trained War Walkers complements this role, disabling enemy firebases before the lightning attack hits home.

BLACK GUARDIAN WAR WALKER SQUADRON

Use the War Walker Squadron entry. However, Black Guardian War Walkers cost 45 points each before weapon upgrades and have BS 4.

BLACK GUARDIAN SUPPORT WEAPON BATTERY

Use the Support Weapon Battery entry. However, Black Guardian Support Weapon Batteries have BS4 and are subject to Tactical Withdrawal. The unit may be joined by a Warlock from the Seer Council or Spear of Khaine.

UK	US	AUSTRALIA	JAPAN	CANADA
Games Workshop Ltd., Willow Rd., Lenton, Nottingham, NG7 2WS.	Games Workshop INC., 6721 Baymeadow Drive, Glen Burnie, Maryland, 21060-6401.	Games Workshop, 23 Liverpool St, Ingleburn, NSW 2565.	Games Workshop Ltd., Willow Rd., Lenton, Nottingham, NG7 2WS.	Games Workshop, 2679 Bristol Circle, Units 2 & 3, Oakville, Ontario, L6H 6Z8.